Our Bond Is Our Gift.
An Interpersonal Look at Relationships

by

Keith "K.L." Belvin

MSHSC, MSED

Bravin Publishing

New York

Copyright © 2018 by K.L. Belvin

All rights reserved. No part of this publication may be reproduced, distributed, or transmitted in any form or by any means, including photocopying, recording, or other electronic or mechanical methods, without the prior written permission of the author or publisher, except in the case of brief quotations embodied in critical reviews and certain other noncommercial uses permitted by copyright law.

Bravin Publishing, LLC
P.O. Box 340317
Rochdale Village, NY 11434
www.bravinpublishing.com

Editor: Shonell Bacon www.chicklitgurrl.com

Graphic Designer: Gregory Graphics http://www.positiv-media.com

Printed in the United States of America

ISBN 978-0-9979441-7-4

Library of Congress Number:

Table of Contents

Dedication ii
Acknowledgments iv
Foreword vi
Introduction x
Anger and Frustration: 1
    Great Motivators for Change
Revealing Your Truth through Transparency 18
The Corruption of Bad Communication 28
When the Rain Won't Go Away: Handling the Bad Days 34
The Importance of Recreating Yourself 42
The Power of Life and Death in a Word 50
Where's the Fruit? Judge a Tree by Its Fruit 62
Fixing Men to Heal Their Relationships 70
Why Are Our Young Men Angry? 88
They Are Still Out There 112
    Part 1: The Good Man 112
    Part 2: The Good Woman 118
Folks Better Work It Out! 128
About the Author 136

i

Dedication

    I dedicate this book to my wife, Tiffany. For without your love and past forgiveness, I wouldn't be in the position I am in to help others with my insight. I want to acknowledge my children Kayelle, Jonathan, Kierra, Anthony, Elijah, Courtney, and Justin. I've given each of you a part of me; I pray it is the best of me. With each of you have some experiences which have allowed this book to touch those who read. I dedicate this book to each person who takes the time to read this book. I pray it helps shine a light on some part of your life. My final dedication is to the Lord. Father God, if you didn't bless me with life and forgiveness of my past sins, I wouldn't be able to help or serve with this book and the words you grant me to help others.

    Special Dedication: To my cousin Phyllis Jones. You won't be here to read this one. You have supported all my work from the beginning. I love you for that. I pray you rest in peace in the bosom of the Lord. "RIP"

K.L. Belvin

Acknowledgments

I want to publicly acknowledge and celebrate Shonell Bacon for her help and assistance while working on the book. I want to say thank you for allowing me to use your intellect and literary talents. Your friendship and professional teaching have helped me grow as a writer. Your role in this book is clear and will be a significant force in the lives we'll change. I pray the Lord continues to bless you in all you do. You are irreplaceable in my life and as a member of the Bravin Publishing literary family. Thank you for all you have done for Bravin Publishing, Tiff and Me.

I also want to celebrate the Beta readers who took the time to read my work and offer their feelings and suggestions with the direction of this book. Continued blessings to Moya and Warren, Tammy, Lisa P, Christine, Dora, Lisa M, and my boy Robert aka Scratch I love you guys.

K.L. Belvin

Foreword

"No man (or woman) is an island entire of itself."
The metaphorical poet John Donne wrote these words in 1623 (minus the parenthetical addition), and they hold true before, during, and after the writing of Donne's essay "Meditation 17." Including NOW.

To live a full life, we must be a part of some form of a relationship. The bonds made within relationships are vital.

Why are relationships, the bonds made, vital?

At the basic level, they are vital because what we do affects others. We might like to think our lives are just for us, and that what we do only affects us, but as the Reverend Dr. Martin Luther King Jr. stated, "Whatever affects one directly, affects all indirectly. I can never be what I ought to be until you are what you ought to be. This is the interrelated structure of reality." Even with people you may never meet or talk to, such as people who drive on the roads with you, how you operate on the highway can affect how they respond to your driving... and vice versa. If your actions can touch them, imagine how your actions (or inactions) might affect a friend, a family member, or a spouse.

Because we know at this base level that we affect one another, we know that we can be either a detriment or a benefit to others. There is a Swedish proverb that goes "Shared joy is a double joy; shared sorrow is half sorrow." When we are connected to others, that bond allows us to strengthen others when they are weak and to be strengthened when we are weak.

When we strengthen each other, we accomplish things, for as former Supreme Court justice Sandra Day O'Connor says, "We don't accomplish anything in this world alone... and whatever happens is the result of the whole tapestry of one's life and all the weavings of individual threads from one to another that creates something."

Relationships allow us to weave our individual threads together to connect, to strengthen and to be strengthened, and to create useful lives for ourselves and others, especially—and hopefully—regarding the legacies, we leave our children.

Relationships, our bonds with others, also—in straightforward and personal ways—affect our faith and our health, too.

Donne told us no person is an island, and even Matthew 18:20 of the Bible (NASB) says

"For where two or three have gathered together in My name, I am there in their midst." This doesn't mean that your solo prayers don't get heard, but fervent prayers of a righteous collective can exact supernatural change!

And that change can be found in our faith—and our health. In the 2012 article "Connect to Thrive" for the website Psychology Today, Dr. Emma M. Seppälä, Ph.D. writes that part of our health 101 basics includes the need to socially connect with others. Doing so, studies have shown, can improve your health, your well-being, and the longevity of your life.

With all the positives for bonding with others, we should all be jumping on board to create healthy, active, long-lasting relationships, right?

OUR BOND IS OUR GIFT

Our bonds within our families, friendships, romantic ties, workspaces, faith, and health transform us to our best—or worst—selves. Because of the latter, a book like Keith L. Belvin's Our Bond Is Our Gift: An Interpersonal Look at Relationships is needed. Through personal experiences, faith, and frank, real talk, Keith breaks down how we can come to the relationship table with a whole self who knows what we want and need and is willing and able to reciprocate those wants and needs to the right people.

I was honored to have worked with Keith in editing and revising this book, but more than that, I was blessed to have had the opportunity to read the book. I am all about self-help and improvement, and Keith offers excellent chapters that tap into understanding things like how anger and frustration can help you and how comfortability can be a detriment. There were many times, especially in the sections on communication and the power of words, when I found myself nodding; saying, "You got me;" and taking notes.

With Our Bond Is Our Gift, Keith has created a book that genuinely crosses into several groups and can be for anybody. If you are at a crossroads in your own life, it's a beautiful book to help you examine where you are, what's working, and how to begin to fix those broken places. If you are married, it's a great book to focus in on areas where you can heighten and tighten your marriage. If you are single, it's perfect for helping you focus on getting self right first then finding and connecting with like-minded potential mates. If you are a parent, you will find information on how to better connect with your children. I'm particularly fond of the chapter "Why Are Our Young Men

Angry?" and how it offers solutions to help black youth where they are now.

If you are a person who needs some healing, and who isn't these days, Our Bond Is Our Gift will have the balm you need. Shonell Bacon,

Author, editor, educator

@ChickLitGurrl

http://chicklitgurrl.com

Introduction

From the live videos I've done using the Facebook and Periscope live streaming platforms over the past few years gave birth to Our Bond Is Our Gift. In my videos, I discuss relationships and people in various ways. As a counselor and mentor, it's my nature and form of ministry to help as many people as possible. This book is designed to touch all who read; this is the same hope I've had for the videos. I work hard to make sure my videos are heartwarming and honest. Transparency is an anchor to who I am since people love to know who they are dealing with or supporting.

A few years back, I thought why not take all these videos and transcribe them into a book. I figured I would set it up for people to be able to read and figure out what's the best way the words within this book could help them. I made the content as clear as I could as I did in my videos to allow more readers to receive the message. I also included questions at the end of the sections for those who wish to dig deeper into the content and *use* the material for their lives.

Typically, this is not the type of book I would write, and I feared it wouldn't be received positively, but I had to remind myself this book comes from a place of transparency. I feel those who will read this book are going to be touched the same way I was when I revealed these thoughts in my original videos. With each video, I hope to reach at least one person to make a connection with, at least one person who will come away from hearing me speak and say, "I get it." I'm hoping a real bond happens to each person who reads this book. I pray it will touch them in a way where they can look inside and consider something they're dealing with and find a way to handle it or, God willing, fix it.

Like any self-help book, the author wants to believe their information is going to be the best information out there. I didn't look at things in that way; I'm merely trying to make sure the information in this book is reflective of my ministry based on the way I mentor and counsel. I am hoping the readers get a feel for my emotional, physical, and spiritual state as I look to transfer it over to them within each chapter.

Enjoy and share with as many people you feel will benefit from the book.
God Bless

Keith "K. L." Belvin MSHSC, MSED

Habakkuk 2:2 New King James Version (NKJV)

The Just Live by Faith

2 Then the Lord answered me and said:

"Write the vision and make it plain on tablets, that he may run who reads it."

Anger and Frustration: Great Motivators for Change

The words "anger" and "frustration" often hold negative connotations. They cause us to frown, to develop severe feelings and equally severe reactions to situations, and they can also push us into depression. We start to feel sad because of the situation we are in, and its understandable.

But here's the thing: anger and frustration can be great motivators.

In the heat of an angry or a frustrated moment, our knee-jerk reactions keep us from seeing this, but it is imperative we stop and catch ourselves.

Let me tell you why.

Short answer: if we don't catch ourselves, we will dwell on the negativity far longer than we need to.

You must cut yourself off and say, "Wait a minute, right now might be the perfect time to start something brand new. This negative situation can be a great thing for me."

Don't laugh. Hear me out. The last thing you probably think of when anger and frustration arise is, "Awesome, let's do something new, exciting, and fun," but this can be the best time to consider something new.

When you look at whatever is causing you anger and frustration, your initial reaction is sadness or borderline depression because nobody likes to be angry and frustrated.

K.L. BELVIN

When we're mad, we act out of character, we say things we don't mean, and we become the worst versions of ourselves.

But there's a practical use for everything which goes on, in, and around the body, including anger and frustration.

As a teacher, I have been in a lot of employment situations where I had to ask myself, "What are you doing?" I began to question myself because anger and frustration would creep in and sit a spell. These negative emotions affected how I thought and how I interacted with everyone around me, and I knew I had to stop letting my emotions affect my reactions. It was then when I was full of these negative feelings I had to take a step back and analyze the cause of my anger and frustration. And you must examine the reasons, too.

If you are angry, frustrated, unfulfilled in your life, the first thing you should do is make a list of those things which might be causing the negative feelings. The very next thing you need to do is ask yourself the following question: *Can I control these things?* So many times, we get angry at things we don't have any control over. If you *can* manage the purpose, then you will want to put into action a plan to fix the problem. Many times, however, the cause is something we can't control. Not having control can make many people feel on edge, nervous, but this is a time for you to step back and relax because you can't do anything about the situation. It's difficult, I know. I'm not claiming you can move a magic wand over the issue and in a flash, it's gone. But this is a perfect time to incorporate some straight truth into the situation. All we can do is what we *can* do. If there is nothing you can do to fix a problem, then your goal should be to do whatever you can in all other matters. If you want to reach your personal promised land, then you need to learn how to separate can-dos from can't-dos and move past negative feelings.

Removing anger and frustration is not easy, but it's doable. Taking time to step back can enable you to consider solutions to dissolve the negative feelings.

One action I use to help eliminate anger and frustration is prayer. I use prayer at moments when I'm angry or mad or at moments when I believe I would do something outside my character. I speak directly to God: "Lord, I will leave this person in your hands because if I say or do anything right now, it's going to cost me. So, I'm just going to sit back and let you take care of it." I know it may sound crazy to those who may not be believers, but that's okay.

Another action you might consider is playing Risk versus Reward. I share this often with my students. I would say to them to "ask yourself if what you're about to do is worth the risk?" Fighting someone might reward you "now," but the bonus from that reward quickly dissipates, leaving you feeling empty and possibly in trouble. I express them they want long-lasting rewards; if the risk is higher than the prize, let it go.

Using your words wisely can also help you push anger and frustration from your mind, especially the words you direct toward yourself. For example, you might say, "I can't help being angry. I'm an angry person in general." No, you're not. You're not an angry person. We're not made to walk around and be mad all the time. You are an individual who is *choosing* to be angry. If you are waking up sore and walking around angry, then know you are doing this because you're not addressing what is causing the anger. You must find the source of your irritation and disconnect from it. Once you do, your anger will dissipate. Instead of using your words to define your negativity, speak light and positivity into yourself. When you talk negatively about yourself, others will react by repeating those words to you, and in return, you become the adversity you describe. Take on the role of someone who is positive, even if it's difficult to do because this is what we are attempting to do. We are trying to make a *positive* change and move forward.

There is always work for us to be doing to make sure we are sound in mind, body, and spirit, and the above three actions can help in developing soundness. However, there is still more work to be done. Once you know the cause of the anger and frustration and realize you *can* control the situation, you need to start replacing the issue with something positive, something which *works* for you.

I've applied these same ideas to situations in my life, especially in my career. In the last ten-plus years, I have grown frustrated with what I have seen in the New York City Department of Education. My first eight years were fantastic, but the last twelve were very difficult. I've had some beautiful times, but I've also had some horrible times. I love the children, but I do not like what the system has become. So instead of being continuously angry and frustrated, I finally decided as much as I love this work, it was time to move and do something else. There were sacrifices, but ultimately, I had to give up this direction in my life so I could do something different, something which would bring me happiness.

<u>Comfortable ≠ Happiness</u>

Comfort cannot be the solution. We cannot try to get rid of anger and frustration just because we want to be comfortable. It must be the pursuit of happiness we strive for because when you achieve whatever happiness means to you, then you will ultimately replace the anger and frustration. You might find your purpose while pursuing your pleasure or you might see it before you take up your new journey. No matter the route, you need to know what's going to make you happy so you can move toward it. For me, I had finally decided to leave New York and move my family to Delaware because I wanted to hit the reset button, and I was going to do some things differently. I was going to create a couple of businesses. I was going to do some things I had wanted to do for me.

Was there a risk? Yes, there was, and I was and am still willing to take the chance because I am a man of faith, and I'm a man who believes in his talent. I'm also a believer in the businesses I'm going to create. Could they fail? Yes, they could, but if they failed, it wouldn't be because I created them. They would fail because I didn't work on them the right way. They would fail because *I* did *not* do what I had to do. Despite the risks, I knew I was not going to keep going into someone's place of employment where they would make money off my work and then give me all types of foolishness and garbage because they felt they could.

I understood business is set up for you to be hired and make less money than the people who hired you. They will let you work for 20 or 30 years and give you a retirement party and possibly a pension, but they're not going to have you make more money than the people who are signing your check. I wanted some of this freedom to myself. So, yes, I walked away from a significant amount of money and left the New York City Department of Education, but I didn't and still don't have a problem with it because I'm doing the things I need to find the happiness that works for me.

Making personal changes was the action I needed to do to put me on the right path to my happiness. You must figure out what your satisfaction level is and what route you need to take to secure it.

Please know frustration and anger don't have to debilitate you. You can use these emotions as your motivators.

So, if we know anger and frustration can be our motivators, then we next need to know what is frustrating us and what is going to make us happy. From there, we need to take the journey to reach a place of content. What is the look of happiness? What is the feeling of joy? Envision yourself in this location. Start to reignite your excitement in the pursuit so when you achieve the satisfaction, it will be so worth it.

Earlier, I mentioned the importance of realizing what you can and can't control and how important it is to act on those things you have control over. You should learn to let go of the things you have no power over. I can't control what's on television, for example; however, I can control what I create and what I can create can get put on TV, and then I will have some say on what I'm trying to offer this world. It might sound a little Pollyannic, but you must be the change you want to see in the world and to do this, you *must change*. Once you understand your frustration and your anger and you choose a different paradigm, a different way of thinking, then it is up to you to decide how you're going to achieve your happiness.

It is important to note when you go on this pursuit of your happiness, you will not be comfortable. If you dislike your job, but always tell yourself things like, "Well, you know my boss is

OUR BOND IS OUR GIFT

not bad" or "Some people have no job," then you are cutting yourself short and dwelling in your comfort. These statements can be true, but if you are not happy and you know you are not living in the active space you need to thrive, comfortability becomes a problem, a slave. So many people expect a person to knock on their door and say, "Hey, here's a million-dollar opportunity. Come and work for me." That comes off great in the movies, but you got to go out there and hustle and grind, and in the pursuit of your happiness, you will come to those things. They will come with pitfalls without question. You may even get hurt in the process, but you have got to be brave enough and surround yourself with people who are supporters of your focus. Often, comfortability will not be your friend in this process.

Believe it or not, comfort is not happiness.

Comfort seems like a great thing. It's an alleviation of pain, of grief, of distress, of feelings. And who wouldn't want to be alleviated of such negative thoughts? If you are grieving and a friend comforts you, its a positive thing. If you are in pain, and medication and prayer support you, these are positive things. If you are stressed and listening to specific songs comforts you, that's a positive thing.

However, if you're in a strained relationship, you're unhappy with your position in life, and you decide to place yourself in "a state of physical ease" as way to settle during these adverse situations, you are then trying to make the situation one of *comfort*, and this is *not* a positive thing.

Comfort *can* create a confident state of mind, but we should not believe comfort equals happiness. Support is something we like to have. We want to be comfortable in what we do, but happiness is an emotion of a whole different level.

In my daily goings-on, I've noticed a lot of people seem to be comfortable at their job, relaxed in their relationship, comfortable with whatever, but in the same breath, they will admit they're not entirely happy, and I don't understand that mindset. We cannot allow comfort to replace happiness because when we do, we're either existing or settling. Either way, just maintaining is not the purpose of life.

Are there times we must settle? Yes. Are there things we must accept? Yes, but it does not mean we stop our pursuit of actual happiness. If you feel you don't have a choice, you must do what you must until opportunities are made available. Ultimately, your pursuit of happiness will drive you to a level of joy. Do not think what you have now is all there is in the world. God has presented us with more than that, so much more. God wants us to obtain much which has nothing to do with personal wealth, but if that is what you think will make you happy, it's out there to be had, as well. No matter which route you choose, you must pursue the journey which makes you happy.

I was speaking to a coworker one day, and she told me she had the necessary education to move forward in her career. When I asked her why she hadn't made moves in that direction, she replied, "I'm comfortable, and I'm not sure if I'm ready to make a move."

It is this embrace of comfortability which causes things to go wrong for us.

OUR BOND IS OUR GIFT

I'm working on creating the life I want, which I believe is going to make me happy. I'm going after it. If I fail, then I'll learn something from it and move forward.

You must believe you can create the life you want. Start by looking in the mirror and asking you "What do I want? What is going to make me happy?" Then generate the plan necessary and get started. Count the costs and get started. A lot of people do the thinking and the planning, but they just can't seem to get into motion. My wife and I were having this conversation, and I told her I was going to help her get to where she wanted to go with the things she wanted to do if that was going to make her happy. I felt it was my job as a husband. If you don't have a husband or a wife, there are still enough people around to help motivate you to get where you need to go.

Comfort or well-being is what preludes being comfortable, yes, and it's okay to be comfortable, but it never compares to true happiness. There isn't much which matches the joy happiness brings. When you are happy with something, when you step out of your comfort zone, and you go for something you are going to love, and you achieve it, it's incredible. Happiness should be our target, and we must find a way to push ourselves past the things which make us contented, which means we must push past the fears of the unknown. To achieve this is where strong personal motivation and external motivation are necessary. First, we must speak positivity into ourselves. We must connect to the positive things surrounding us and start our journey toward obtaining a connection of both to our daily lives. Let's look at the characters in *The Lord of the Rings*. They had a track, a purpose. They came together, decided on the journey, and took the journey head-on. There were certain pitfalls along the way. Significant roadblocks, too, but they thought with the end goal in mind. The *end* was their motivation.

When I went back to school to work on my second master's degree, my motivation was graduation. I had some people ask me why I would need a second degree. I could just use the first one. Well, I was using the first one, but the second one was going to help me lay the foundation of the new plan I was making once I left teaching. Instead of listening to the naysayers or my doubt, I focused on my end game: graduation. I thought about walking across the stage in my cap and gown and having my wife and daughter in the audience, proud of me.

Having an active endgame helps you to eliminate frustration and anger from your journey. Don't get me wrong, frustration and anger are lovely starting points because you don't have to belabor them once you get started on your trip. Once you begin to move in your new direction, you don't have to worry about what made you angry or frustrated. Your focus is on the goal at hand.

I mentioned pitfalls and roadblocks. They are inevitable, and when they come, you will think you have failed. And you know what? Even if you did fail, it would be OK because failure is part of the journey, too. The goal is to not dwell on the stumble. Failure is momentary. Well, it can be if you stand, turn toward your goal, and move forward. Staying in the center of your inability, reliving it, and thinking about it is your choice. The moment of failure has already passed. Right Now, your present positioning, is what's important. When I coached young adults, the best lessons were after the losses we suffered. Seeing them all emotional, I would say, "Hold on, hold on, stop all the emotion because we aren't going to let the team beat us twice. Yes, they beat us on the scoreboard, but we aren't going to let them hit us emotionally. We're going to hold our heads up; we are going to shake their hands because we only ran out of time. They got us today, okay. We are going to learn from this, figure out what we did wrong, and do better. But we are not going to continue to harp on the loss because now they are continually beating us, and the game has ended."

At the next practice, I wouldn't bring up the score. I would bring up things we needed to improve on instead. For them, I used failure as a kick in the behind to move forward. Failure is the part you don't want, and when it occurs, it's already out the way. I didn't want it; I got it, now let's move forward. Think with the goal in mind; the goal has to be the motivator; the goal has to be "I could care less about frustration and anger. I'm after joy, the joy of when I get there. The joy of when I've done it."

The one thing I love about certain reality shows is where people start off. Often, they start with a tremendous obstacle to overcome. On *The Biggest Loser*, for example, the contestants begin with a statement like "I thought it was impossible to lose weight," but through using a trainer and personal motivators, they meet their weight goal, overcome a consistent obstacle, and find brand-new confidence in themselves. For me, the best part of it all is the look of joy. *It is that* look, that place of ultimate calm, and peace are what we should be striving to achieve. We must work towards the goal of owning that look and feel.

Another example comes from the movie *The Pursuit of Happiness*. In the film, Will Smith plays the role of Chris Gardner, a man going through some ups and downs in his life with his son. I use the movie in my life to ramp up my motivation when it needs boost forward. In the film, there are two scenes where I want you to focus your attention.

The first is where Will Smith has nowhere to sleep for the night because there were no more beds at the shelter. He decides to stay in a subway bathroom with his son. While sitting on the floor with his son sleeping between his legs, someone knocks at the door attempting to enter. The only thing Smith thinks to do is put his foot out to block the door from opening. At that moment, it was his only concern. He wasn't worried about money, his job, or anything of that nature. He was concerned about getting through that moment and his son's well-being. This focused urgency is often missing in many of lives.

When I counsel men of all ages, I use this scene and ask, "What do you think the Will Smith is thinking at this exact moment?" I'll get answers like, " He doesn't want the guy to come inside the bathroom," He's scared.", And a few other ideas are tossed out. I'll then reply, "Okay, but think deeper, what else do you consider he's thinking?" In helping the men dig deeper into the scene, I offer my thoughts. I ask them to focus on that particular moment and on what Will Smith singular worry was getting through the night. The only thing on Smith's mind was how was he going to get through this night with his son be his actions to this point in the movie was on the more significant goal he was after. He needed to do whatever was necessary to make it through till morning to get back into the mix of what was his current mission. Smith's situation is something many of us have never faced, so we don't look inward for the answers to serious problems when attempting to pull ourselves or our family through. Every time I watch this movie, I am moved to my core with Smith's portrayal of determination and his attention on his son because it's a testament to the strength and focus during trying times we all have or will face in our lives. Will Smith's character understands he had to do something to change his current circumstances if his life was going to be different.

The second scene I want you to pay attention to is towards the end. At this part of the movie is the part which drives it all home for me and often the men I've shown the film too. The heart touching moments occurs in the last five or six minutes of the movie. After being summoned into the big boss's office; Smith doesn't have an idea why. The top boss, with a minimal expression on his face, tells him, "Nice Shirt" before asking him to sit. He is referring to the first time they met Smith. At that moment Smith still has no clue why he's there in the office. Smith replies, "Yes. I thought I would wear a shirt today being the last day and all." Harking back to when he came for the interview with just a tee-shirt and jacket due to a personal problem on the day he was to meet the bosses. He's also referring to it being the last day of a grueling internship which has forced Smith to work for no pay. A professional opportunity has been his mission from the moment he accepted the chance at gaining the only opening the company gives to its top applicant. Up to this point, Smith has been killing himself for the position. The boss says to Smith, "Okay, we appreciate that. But wear one tomorrow, OK? Because tomorrow is going to be your first day if you'd like to work here as a broker?" It's at this moment Smith's character realizes all his hard work has paid off. He got the one position out of all the people who were there fighting throughout the internship. At this moment is where I beg the men to pay attention. I know for me, Smith sells the scene so well you have no choice but to get pulled into the moment. It is the feeling from the scene I am relying on to reach inside those who are watching and pull out their humanity. It's my way to get them to want joy for themselves. The boss asks Smith's "Was it easy?" Tears fall from Smith's face as he replies, "No it wasn't." Smith's reaction moves me and motivates me every time I see this part. I have seen it have the same effect on men who didn't know they could feel this way or refused to allow themselves. The boss has no idea what Smith's character has gone through to get to this point. But we do, from being the fly on the wall to Smith's journey to this moment. Smith had to do yeoman's work to put him in position to get the job.

 When we live in a state of comfortability, we don't get the chance to obtain our goals like Smith's character was able to. To secure the complete happiness, you must fight to achieve satisfaction. Smith narrates this fact as he leaves the building to celebrate his triumph to himself quietly in the middle of a crowded sidewalk. The happiness we see is what we all can claim if we're willing to place ourselves into the fire to forge into something new the world has never seen.

OUR BOND IS OUR GIFT

The following are self-reflection questions to journal your thoughts or to sit and think about the content in this chapter. Give yourself a quiet space to read, think, and write on these matters. And be honest with yourself. Honesty and transparency is the key to you getting to your best self.

<u>Self-Reflection</u>

Anger and Frustration: Great Motivators for Change / Self-Reflection

This chapter offers many things for you to think about, and it is crucial for you to unpack each facet to examine how they relate to you right now.
The first facet this chapter tackles is the importance of self-reflection. Sit and think about all the things currently going on in your life. Good, bad, and in-between.

1. In your self-reflecting, reflect on the word anger. Are there any issues in your life which ignite this feeling in you? If so, name these problems individually. Ask yourself what is causing the aggression with each point. Ask yourself if there is some cog of the issue you could use to motivate you in a positive direction.

2. Anger and frustration often go together. Because of this, questions posed in #1 can be utilized here for frustration, too.

3. Think about any of the issues which might be causing you both anger and frustration. What problems can you control? Honestly. Is there something you can do right now or something you could do in small increments over time to fix a

problem? Remember; work on the issues you can. Give the others over to God and keep moving forward.
4. Comfortability isn't always a good thing, as this chapter articulated. Sometimes, we get stuck where we are. We can't dig ourselves up, and out of the hole, so we just make do. How comfortable are you in your life? Are you doing some things just to "make do"? Are there people, places, and things keeping you in this comfortable space? If there is comfortability in your life, think about whether this is good or stagnant comfortability.

5. What does happiness mean to you? What would you have to do to obtain the level of joy achieved by Smith in the film? In your pursuit of happiness, you need to be able to visualize what happiness means to you, focus on the goal of achieving satisfaction, and find the motivation to continue your pursuit

OUR BOND IS OUR GIFT

Revealing Your Truth through Transparency

The last chapter focused on how anger and frustration can be great motivators for change. As the examples showed, this is the case for you dealing with issues which involve your increase as an individual *and* your growth as part of a relationship. In addition to finding ways to turn anger and frustration into positives, you must also learn to be transparent.

To be in any healthy relationship, you must be transparent.

Too often, we allow our previous experiences to dictate how we move and act in a relationship; you cannot allow that to take place. Instead of reviving and re-enacting the negatives of a prior relationship, you need to learn from them, so you are better equipped to handle a good, healthy, lasting relationship.

And when you do find the person whom you want to be with in a lasting relationship, you need to practice transparency. Put your truth out there. It might hurt initially to hear the truth, but if you do not show who you are, you're living a lie, and your relationship will not have the stability it needs and deserves.

Transparency not only helps you, but it also helps the person whom you are in a relationship because, for one thing, your mate will be able to see similarities between the two of you. Transparency allows you and your partner to stand on solid ground, to become mutual visionaries in your future together.

OUR BOND IS OUR GIFT

When I told *my truth* in my book *From Gigolo to Jesus*, it was cathartic and necessary for me to release inner demons. My revelations were shocking for so many, and I knew they would be, but for me to be better, for me to be whole, I needed to show the good, the bad, and the very ugly.

In the book, I stated the number of women I had been with sexually. I was a nasty man, having been with somewhere between three-hundred to four-hundred women. Many remind me I was disgusting, and I agreed. I regret all the liaisons with those women, who now, because of my lack of self-control, have a practical understanding of what my wife and I share romantically in our bedroom. Sadly, I cannot go back and change it, so it must be used as motivation to remain faithful and reason to prevent others from doing the same. I can only live in the current and focus on the future if I am going help others. One of the things you quickly realize as you mature is the past is what it is, and it cannot change. My wife knows every dirty detail of my history. I put it out to the world in the book because I am not allowing anyone to attempt to come from my past and derail anything I have in place now in my life.

In my goal of being transparent, I discuss how I reached a place where I would think any of the things I did was okay. I spent a significant amount of time on the streets. My mother and grandmother did the best they could to raise a man; however, I had no male role models during this time. I looked up to the men in the streets who were guiding me as they knew, and their primary lessons were to see women as objects. What I've learned is when you cannot see a human as a human; you can and will do anything to them. I did not see women as mutual partners. I saw women as conquests. They were toys for me to use when playing. Once I matured and turned my life around, I apologized as much as I could. When I

K.L. BELVIN

wrote my book *From Gigolo to Jesus*, it was to be transparent with where I was with my life, to make a personal statement. My spiritual focus is what pushes me to work as hard as I do because I believe I owe the Lord and the world for past behaviors. There was a time I felt I didn't owe anyone else. Why? Because I thought I could have died at any moment at the hands of someone else, or God could have just said enough with this and snuffed my life out for the way I treated people. Now, I feel I owe an apology to anyone I haven't gotten a chance to speak to from my past. My current focus is to help men, young and older, to choose the path I eventually did. Serving others is another reason I must be transparent. It is my transparency people can see themselves and accepts the healing I'm offering. When you lay your garbage out there and say, "I'm going to let you see it all as it is," people will sift through my past and say, "Oh my God, Keith's garbage was as bad as mine." The bond created is where I rely on my transparency to illuminate a path for them.

When you and your significant other are transparent with each other, and you now start to fuse together a mutual vision, you will begin to feel and see things you did not even know existed. Mutuality explains why people who are genuinely in love do not seem to care about what is going on in the world. And why individuals who apparently not tend to hate those who are in love. To them, the loving couple seems so damn happy. They are. I know, because my wife and I are.

When you have overcome foolishness, negativity, and filth, you cannot beat the cleanliness and love which comes from a stable relationship. I do not care how many women I have been with; nothing beats sitting on the couch with my wife watching a movie while our daughter runs back and forth without care or the nights we go to hang out and grab something to eat. Nothing comes close to someone passing by you and kissing you on your forehead before they go to bed and ask what time you are coming to bed. Nothing beats when she cuddles up next to me and puts her arm around my shoulder when I am sleeping; it is her way of checking if I am there and expressing her security. You see, a person can lie down with as many men or women as you want, but the love which derives from an honest, warm, loving embrace is unbeatable. This stability happens when you are completely transparent with your partner.

Real love causes transparency to be like a warm coat on a cold day. Now imagine you're inside that jacket saying, "No one is taking this coat away from me. I am not taking this off until I reach home. I do not care what anyone says. I am good!"

Love is this way, when we are transparent. The crazy part is many of us are not willing to be overtly clear because we are fearful of things which have happened in the past and thinking it's going to happen again or we'll be judged by our partners. We fail to realize our constant overthinking on the past may just recreate itself in our present.

Transparency is the foundation of all relationships. So many of us look back on failed relationships and wonder why things did not work. We wonder what was wrong with us, or we take the arrogant role and believe there was nothing wrong with us?

But take a second and think.

How transparent are you? How open have you been in the past?

Ladies, are you trying to judge the new man because of the old mistakes you made with the men from your past.

Men, are you doing the same with ladies you meet? A beautiful woman might be standing *right* in front of you, but you are unable to see her because she's wearing the same perfume as your cheating ex-girlfriend. Because you have not gotten real, become transparent with yourself over your past relationship, something as small and silly and trivial as perfume can keep you from *seeing* a woman who could be your perfect mate.

Not realizing the old mistakes, you made, not understanding how a *scent* puts you in a contrary position with a possible mate—these are potential issues which can arise when you are not transparent.

You must stop and see if you are putting out what it is you are trying to attract. Are you open to your wishes? What are you willing to give and not give? Where are you in your life right now? If you're still hurt, be honest and obvious about it. If a person is attracted to someone, but they are dealing with emotions from a previous relationship, my suggestion is, to be honest about where you are in your life at the moment. I ask clients to be open and truthful about the things they would like to see in their significant other and what they're still dealing with if anything. In doing so, we can begin to shovel trash to the side and get to the heart of the matter. The vulnerability is not a weakness; it just means you have an area which needs work. Over time I've learned people do not know how to release their pain. These feelings touch deep-rooted nerves, and many don't understand how to handle the emotions if not guided correctly and with support.

When talking to hurt females who are suffering from the pains of previous relationships, I always say, "Sister, please do not allow a man who did you dirty to continue to hurts your days and years after the fact." Do not keep paying the price for past foolishness. What he did to you then, he did, but if you are still holding on to it weeks, months, years later, you are in turn hurting yourself. He is not bothering you anymore. You are beating yourself up by using his name, and it is fraudulent behavior which offers no chance of healing.

OUR BOND IS OUR GIFT

And if you are hurting, guess what? It is okay. Pain is pain. It doesn't release itself overnight. However, if you know you are not ready for another relationship because you are in pain, then be honest about it. You are not going to fall victim to anything by saying I just do not think I can be the best partner to you right now. But you also must understand by saying that, he or she may walk away, and you must be okay with the departure. You cannot try to hold a real person to play because you are still working on you. You must be transparent and honest.

One beautiful thing about the relationship my wife and I have is we're very transparent with each other because we want the relationship to continue to do well. We don't just sit around and know our relationship will work itself out on its own. We put in the active work. Even with our disagreements, we are transparent. If something seems to be bothering her, I'll ask, "What's the matter with you?" I don't ask to be disrespectful; it is because I need her. She might answer me now, or she might take a day and come back and say, "Okay, this is what I had an issue with." We deal with it because if you are not transparent, the muddy issues you fling onto your windows will eventually glue those windows shut.

If you are not where you want to be in your relationship, take a good look at yourself. To be what you say you want, you must be prepared to give. Having a good relationship isn't a thing of luck. You can't control fate, but you can control how you act and what you say while in your relationship. When you put the work in, the results will be positive because of your efforts. I learned it. I had to screw up my first marriage to learn how to make the second one work. I am trying to help people and prevent them from going the same route. I want to see people not make the mistake of giving away years to someone and then realizing it is not working.

K.L. BELVIN

If you are going to try to start a relationship with someone, you should believe you both have reached the point in your individual lives where transparency is critical. If you are honest, a real man or woman will see the honesty in you because they understand your current situations. When you know who you are and what you need and can state those things to a potential mate, you illustrate transparency and are more than likely going to receive it. For example, a female might say to a prospective partner, "I am working, going to school, and I have children. My time is significant to me, and I don't like spending it on frivolous things which will go nowhere." Being this transparent takes the pressure off the female. She stated her truth, so all she can do is accept the response and move on. The potential mate, having heard her truth, can tell her he's just interested in dating people and they part ways, or he can respond, "I get that. What days you have off? What time would be good for us to see each other?" He will work with the female to spend time together because he saw her truth and is still interested in getting to know her.

Aside from the significant benefit of speaking your truth and not having major past issues hanging over you, transparency is excellent at cutting through foolishness. The example above clearly illustrates this. If the female didn't speak the truth, she risks falling into a relationship which doesn't fit her needs, and like many people, she could end up staying in the relationship for years because of her inability to cut ties. What keeps the female from falling into evil traps is not just the ability to be transparent; it's also the capacity to *stand firm in your transparency*. You cannot tell someone your truth then allows them to manipulate you, control you, and make you forget who you are and what you want and need. You must *know your truth* and *speak your truth on the solid ground*.

OUR BOND IS OUR GIFT

Transparency does not mean you are to be rude or ignorant to others. It doesn't say you are negating other's feelings. Transparency means you are stating what you need in the hope of receiving openness, attraction, and acceptance from others for building strong, lasting relationships.

If you put the best efforts into living your best life through being transparent, you will suffer fewer disappointments because when those disappointments occur, you will be quicker to realize the person or thing you wanted is not for you. Do not be afraid to reveal your truth. Do not leave anything on the table. Do not allow doubt to stop you from putting stuff out there. Be who you are supposed to be, let a person see it, and then go from there.

The following are self-reflection questions to journal your thoughts or to sit and think about the content in this chapter. Give yourself a quiet space to read, think, and write on these matters. And be honest with yourself. Honesty and transparency is the key to you getting to your best self.

Self-Reflection

Bonding with Transparency

Honesty, transparency is the key to you getting to your best self.

Being transparent is scary. When you reveal your true self, you can receive immediate negative feedback from people, and who wants that? But what we learn in this chapter is life isn't about what people think of you. It's about being truthful to who you are so the relationships you build with others start on a firm ground of understanding.

1. Who are you? Honestly. Take a moment to think about "the fly on the wall." What if this fly followed you throughout the day, taking in how you speak to yourself and others, how you carry yourself, how you think about yourself and others. How would that fly define you if it were to share the info collected?

2. Now, you have assessed, determined who you are, ask yourself: is this what you are? Are there people, places, and things, past events have crafted you into who you are now? Many times, the heaviness of the world and situations can cover our truth and have us believing lies in our reality. What facets of your response to #1 are real? Which are false?

3. How can you work to develop further, thus increase, the positive aspects of who you are?

4. How can you work to eliminate the negative issues of who you are?

5. If you are currently in a relationship, think about how transparent you are with your significant other. Do you communicate your feelings and concerns? Does your mate know what you want and need and expect? The flip side of this is also to examine what you're getting from your partner. What can you do (or continue to do) to keep your mate being transparent with you?

6. If you are currently single, examine your responses to questions 1 through 4. How can developing an open nature help you in finding the right person for you? Now, you under-

OUR BOND IS OUR GIFT

stand the importance of transparency, what might you now look for when opening yourself up to a possible mate?

The Corruption of Bad Communication

1 Corinthians 15:33 (KJV) – "Be not deceived: evil communications corrupt good manners."
"Evil (Bad) communication corrupts good manners (character)."

We can agree communication is critical for transparency, right? It is crucial to communicate our wants, needs, and desire efficiently, so we receive the things we seek.

We can also agree not all communication is virtuous. As we are developing our character and assessing who we are and what we want, we need to be mindful of understanding the differences in good and evil communications.

In checking to make sure communication is right, you want first to review the credentials of the person who's speaking to you. Look at them and see if they are using the information they are giving to you and make sure their reasoning makes sense. There have been times when I'm talking to someone and ask them, "Where did you get your information?" Their response will be, "My partner." And I sit back and think, *well, isn't your partner broke*, or *isn't your partner angry*, or *isn't your partner locked up*. You have got to look at the source because not all information is useful information, and we know this, and it's a straightforward premise.

One of the reasons we don't follow up on information received is we allow our hearts to get in the way. We say, "Well,_____ is my friend" or "'____ is my coworker," or "'___ is somebody whom I care about." Just because you care about them does not mean you must listen to their advice. Not every sympathetic shoulder can help you. In fact, sometimes it's not a sympathetic shoulder you need. Sometimes it's a swift kick in the behind, and the people around us may not give it to us if we're not checking. We must be careful of the information we let in because bad communication affects the good character. Some Bible verses say good *moral* character, so a lot more is at stake than we think. Your character is everything; your moral system is everything. If the people around us are feeding us negative information, then our moral system is at risk, our character is in danger. You must double, triple, quadruple check what information you're getting. We tell our kids the importance of not following everyone, then why as adults are we not doing the same thing? We say to our children, "If Jimmy jumped off the bridge, are you going to jump off with him?" We don't check our friend the same way until it is too late.

  To avoid letting in corrupt communication, we also must watch what we're choosing to use to entertain ourselves. Not all entertainment is harmful to people for the same reasons, but we all must still be careful. If I am at a right place in my life, I could watch a television show and not be swayed by it at all. However, if you are a person who is influenced or moved quickly, then you should select carefully with personal discernment because you don't want your character or moral system to be affected. Same applies to music. I can listen to specific music to examine the lyrics because I'm trying to debunk the words, so I know how to present the song to kids or other adults. I'm not a conspiracy theorist, but I see conspiracies exist, so when I'm watching a television show or listening to a song, the minute I hear something, I stop and write thoughts down. We're not supposed to be sponges, merely sopping up what entertainment gives us. We're expected to critique. If we don't, we might absorb the negative into our spirit, beginning a moral and character assassination.

I have a friend who teaches an introductory course in mass communication. One goal of the course is to get first-year college students to critique the media they consume. With our 24-7 news cycle and the growth of "social media as news," many of our youth see a tweet or Facebook post as truth. They don't take the time to find sources to verify information. They quickly retweet and share content, and if the material is false—therefore, evil communication—all they do is continue the lie. Not verifying information for self says a lot about each student; being willing to share the deceptions gives their audience ammunition to judge them negatively.

We must be vigilant in scrutinizing all information which is pushed towards us, and when we come across communication which oddly stirs a contrary position within us, we need to distance ourselves and let others know why the connection is not right for us. Whether the scrutiny is telling your friend to stop speaking about "X" because it doesn't line up with your morals or by turning off the TV when a specific show comes on, we must do something.

And of course, this sounds far easier than it is. Many of us have grown up in environments where we didn't learn to discern between good from evil communication, and as a result, we find it difficult to deal with specific conversations in our adult lives. The lack of auditory nurturing affects us in our adult lives. I see this all the time because as an educator I know children who are damaged, and I know they were not born that way. When I say damaged, I'm speaking about their behavior. Immediately, I think of the adults in the child's life and think no one is checking what the child is saying or how he or she acts. The only thing left to happen is for that child to be led down a path which is going to destroy them morally because right now at six, seven, or eight years old, they don't even realize what is coming out of their mouth is vile. Because of the lack of proper nurturing, lousy communication has affected a child's morals. It is just simple.

How many of us sit back quietly when we hear conversations we know are just ridiculous. We don't put our foot down because we don't want to be considered the negative person, we don't want people to call us the bible thumper, we don't want people to call us whatever insulting religious label they put in place.

If corrupt communication affects character or morals or both, depending on which version of the Bible you read, you must consider if what you're currently hearing is worth the risk. There is no reason to take the chance with unsure people when there are billions of people in the world you could align yourself with. This corruption doesn't just go for the communication we let *in through listening*; this is especially important to the conversations we have. What does it say about our character and morals if we are the ones spewing hate and negativity? We must be guards of our mouths, so we communicate peace, happiness, and positivity.

The following are self-reflection questions to journal your thoughts or to sit and think about the content in this chapter. Give yourself a quiet space to read, think, and write on these matters. And be honest with yourself. Honesty and transparency is the key to you getting to your best self.

Self-Reflection

Bonding with Good Communication

Who we get our advice from can often reflect our success and failure in the endeavors we pursue. As mentioned earlier in this chapter, the Bible states: "evil (bad) communications corrupt good manners (character)." Getting the wrong information from others can not only destroy your character but also destroy facets of your life, such as relationships and careers.

1. What does "bad communication" mean to you?

2. Who do you often go to for advice?

3. In considering your "advisors" from #2, who of these people often give you good advice? Who usually gives you wrong information?

4. What type of entertainment do you partake in: consider books, TV shows, movies, songs, websites, videos, etc.?

5. Does any of the entertainment you engage in have negative connotations?

6. If your answer to #5 is yes, what are those negative connotations? How do they affect who you are and what you do? How can you eliminate these forms of entertainment, so you can illuminate your best self?

7. What have you told yourself which may create adverse personal communication? Just as we should guard our mind, body, and spirit from the evil interaction of others, we should also defend ourselves against ourselves. If you find you are often your own worst enemy, how can you work to do away with the unscrupulous communication or turn it into useful contact?

When the Rain Won't Go Away: Handling the Bad Days

I am not the first person to say this, but it bears a repeat: in any relationship, you will deal with both good and bad times. Our goal is to learn how to accept both.

It doesn't mean you must enjoy bad times, but you must learn how to deal with these times because they are character builders. They are moments which can destroy relationships because values can become pits, and those holes can become cavernous if you don't deal with them.

When you've reached a decline in any relationship, you must first recognize there is a decline, and then you need to put in the work to figure out how to get the relationship back on an incline. The more time you allow a situation to decline, the higher chance you have of never being able to fix the situation.

Again, just like I've been saying, this is not necessarily easy to do. It is so effortless to give in to the negativity because our first inclination when conflict occurs is to run and hide, so silence and lack of communication become things we don't have a problem embracing. We become quiet, and we tend to find other things to do, see, hear to take our minds off the situation. For some people, drug use or drinking alcohol is the preferred way of dealing; with others, this can come from talking to people who feed them with negative information or people who might become closer than your mate, leaving you to commit adultery. For others, speaking to everyone in a negative way is their choice of coping. The things we say to ourselves when things go badly, such as, "I knew this relationship wouldn't last," "I know s/he's going to cheat on me," "S/he doesn't understand me and probably hates me now for not speaking my mind." Remember, our words speak life or death into our lives. If we use bad communication (with ourselves) to handle a situation, nothing good can come from it. The reaction doesn't have to be as relationship-ending as the ones mentioned above, but any response which doesn't include dealing with the conflict is a bad response to a bad situation. When we handle a bad situation with a bad attitude, and we do it long enough, we may even fall into the comfortability of negativity. We say things like, "Well, this is what I deserve," or "I'll never find happiness, so I might as well stay in this."

What is so vital to know and then to remember during times like this is **life is not like that**.

We have to be bold enough to step outside of the dangerous situation and say, "I don't like where I am in my life. I want to get back to the good times." Then, we must be bold enough to say this to our mate. And we must be brave enough to listen and not overreach when our partner says these things to us. When they reach out, it's your job to say, "I got you."

You may have heard the following statement before: "Life is what you create." And this is true because there are going to be disappointments, but you can't control them. You can, however, control how you feel about the frustrations and how you react to them.

Say you wake up on the wrong side of the bed and predict you're going to have a bad morning. Instead of staying in a place of negativity, attach your thoughts to what you're going to do that afternoon or evening. Yes, I'm making it sound simplistic, but really, often it's the simplest things are difficult for us to say and do. Even if you are facing devastating news, this, too, can be overcome emotionally. You must believe you can make the changes. However, it may take longer for you.

And here's the thing, no matter how easy or difficult it is for you to make the changes: they must be done.

Why?

Because when we suppress, the suppression doesn't last long. Luke 8:17 states "For there is nothing hidden that will not be disclosed." We often hear this scripture in the following way: *What's done in the dark will always come to light.* Everything you suppress will show its self in some form or fashion. And often, it's revealed in a way that hurts you and others.

You may not be able to control your situation, but you can control how you feel. For example, instead of lamenting on the negatives, you could get up and thank God for the images. Doing so puts *you* in control of the situation. We must understand, no matter how bad the situation is, God allowed it for a reason. We don't like to think like that because we want to believe all the right things and blessings come from God. Sometimes, the negativity placed on us comes from God, and if we look deep enough inside, we'll see God also gave us the means to get through it. When you do take a look inward and use what God gave you, you'll be a better person and be able to help others deal. If you don't believe you are internally secure, and then you should look externally for things which can help, keeping in mind you are looking for things which offer sound counsel and excellent communication.

We like to think we can handle all things on our own, but even the Bible states we can control all things through Christ who strengthens us. He enhances not only us but also those people, places, and things which come into our lives for good. To receive the goodness, we must realize we are not monolithic entities. We are humans, destined to communicate

OUR BOND IS OUR GIFT

and connect, to help and to be helped. We must open our mouths and speak when we're in a dangerous situation. Communication is key. When you have negative days, you don't just fold it up inside and say, "I'll deal with it." There will be things greater than you, and you'll have to say to somebody, "Please help me." Even if the first person says no, we must continue to search for the things we know will help.

God is one of the most significant resources. When you start to read scriptures, you will notice so many stories you can relate to and be the object of learning. When someone says they can't help you, it's not a negative. Continue the journey. Faith in self, and for many in God, is needed to reach higher heights. We pay a lot of lip service instead of action. It is when things are right we say, "God is good, and God is great." When we are shattered and battered, we should go "Thank you, God" so when people ask why the praise, we can say "Because he trusted me enough to give it to me, and if he did, he's going to show me how to fight." When you do, people will gravitate to you and will want to listen to you. They'll want to know how you dealt with it and got past it.

I know you might be thinking I'm making this sound so easy, but I don't know anything in life which is obtained effortlessly. We must make a way if you want to achieve. You have control of your emotional and spiritual aspects. It all comes down to your belief and your faith if you claim to have it. Even if you're not a person of faith, you can still look your situation in the face and say this is a starting point. Too often, my brothers and sisters will beat you over the head with scriptures, but scripture is a foreign language to a person who's not connected to the church. What many Christian brothers and sisters need to consider is how we can get people to apply what they're asking for without having to use scriptures exclusively. Here's my question to you: do the people you're speaking to understand where your mind and heart is with your offer of assistance? Are heart and soul connected to the proposal? You can't believe in God with your heart and not your account. If your report says, "I believe in God," then your heart must say, "I believe this is not the endpoint of a person's life and people can change. This change can happen when people come to a deeper understanding of themselves. God doesn't care about what you want. He has plans for each person on the planet." We must alert people to this fact to help with personal transformation. The question becomes what you are going to do now?

When I first came home at 32, separated and pending divorce, I fell upon a bed and asked myself how I could be back home after leaving, getting married, and having children? How could I have failed so epically?

My grandmother opened the door and said, "Cry tonight and then get your ass up and start living. We didn't raise you soft, and God didn't make you soft."

H advice helped jump start my life. I've done more since getting divorced from my first wife than I did when I was with her. It all goes back to that moment on the bed. Who knew my grandmother's advice would become a starting point for my new productive life as a recently single man? I didn't. I couldn't see it as I was caught up in my emotions.

You must have rain. Take it away, and things will happen to the planet. The question is how you will react to it? How do you respond to your negative situation or your pain? Your pain is not unique. What is unique is you and how you choose to let the world understand how individual you are.

The question is can you get out of the hole you're in at this point in your life?

The short answer: YES.

OUR BOND IS OUR GIFT

You start climbing, scratching, and digging to get out. You fight to make sure the hole does not keep you in place. You start making waves in this world and refuse to allow your situation to become a bubble. Watch how others gravitate to you.

In *Kung Fu Panda 2*, the peacock says to the panda; *I took from you everything. You should be broken. I took your parents from you. How did you find peace? I wounded you.*

The panda replies, *No, you didn't. You must let all stuff from the past go. It just doesn't matter. Wounds heal.*

I paraphrase, but the sentiment remains the same.

Kids may see that scene and not understand the deeper meaning, but we adults should see the message. The panda was saying the peace he gained occurred because he accepted his past, and in his acceptance, he found inner peace. Inner peace creates strength outwardly. When you internally allow God to grant you order, you become stronger on the outside. When adverse situations happen, you endure; grow better, and in the end stronger. This is the underlining factor of faith on its own.

People often ask me how I hold up against the different negativity I've faced in my life. I tell them it's not me; it's God. The minor road is narrow and treacherous; God said that. When you take the risky path, you must walk through the valley of the shadow of death, but you will fear no evil. God tells you not to worry. Process the information for a second. The underlining question to you is, do you continue to believe in your most significant time of dismay? Can you close your eyes and say "God, you've got me, let's go"? When you travel the treacherous road, it is what needs to happen. Many of us are unable do that because we want the easy way, we don't want to face any pain or worry.

Get up and live life. Get your butt up and lean on the God you believe in. But if God is not your focus, get up and learn to lean on the talents you have inside you. There are times you must push yourself to be a better you to get out of a situation. Remember no lousy day lasts forever. You do not have to stay in a negative place physically, mentally, or spiritually. I've seen people who can't let go of any negatives in their lives. I always ask what they gain by holding on to pain or continually checking on a person who no longer considers them. You must take a step back, look at the situation, and ask, "Where am I in this?" Then it's time to put a plan into motion. Everything is an opportunity to learn.

We need rain. It is a part of life. No matter the storm we're dealing with, it won't last forever. You have control of your emotional state. Do not allow your current circumstances to dictate how you feel spiritually and emotionally. Remember you can keep yourself focused. You must thank the Lord for the problems because He will help you through and out of them. He will send supporters and motivators. You must trust him in the bad times.

Below are self-reflection questions to journal your thoughts or to sit and think about the content in this chapter. Give yourself a quiet space to read, think, and write on these matters. And be honest with yourself. Honesty and transparency is the key to you getting to your best self.

Self-Reflection

Bonding with the Good and Bad Days

OUR BOND IS OUR GIFT

Every one of us will deal with good and bad days. This is not an opinion.

It is a straight fact.

Because of this, we need to be equipped with dealing with all the days we encounter. If we know we will experience ups and down, then our goal should be to combat the evil days and celebrate the good ones.

1. Take a moment to list every positive thing about you.

2. If you are in a relationship, what are positive things about your mate and your relationship?

3. If you are single, what are positive things you can bring to the table in a relationship?

4. The positive things you thought of for questions 1 through 3 should become mantras, things you say to yourself (in mind or aloud) every day so the more you have them in your mind, the more you will come to believe and accept them.

5. How can you celebrate the good days – for yourself and your relationship?
6. When wicked days occur, how do you react? Think of how a bad day typically affects you individually and as a mate. Are there adverse reactions you can eliminate or turn into positive effects?

The Importance of Recreating Yourself

Have you ever found yourself in a rut? You know; it seems like you only exist? You do the same thing, day in and day out, and you don't feel growth, excitement, a zest for life.
Don't worry. Most of us have been there.
And many of us remain there.
Why?
That dreaded word: comfortability. Change is scary because it has no guarantee, and many of us want the guarantee things will be better once we've completed the transformation. So, instead of overcoming the fear, instead of changing, we dwell in the comfort of existing.

We cannot be afraid to change, to recreate ourselves. And we cannot fear those who might not understand our need to recreate. When I began my second master's degree, someone asked me why I would go for the second one at 48. They started to run through their thoughts on what direction I could've gone and questioned why I went in the direction I did. I respected their opinion and thought about it, but I was recreating me. I was walking away from 20 years of teaching, and I wanted to do something different, so I decided to work on a degree in human services with a specialization in counseling and ministry. It may not fit or be to the likes of everyone, but I can't worry about that because I am recreating me.

If you are looking to embark on your recreation, here is a short guide of steps to help you on your journey.

Step One: Get past the fear. You cannot recreate yourself if you are afraid of letting go of the person you are now. Know now you will face scary moments, but through the actions you make, you will test your mettle and grow.

Step Two: Complete a self-assessment. Examine *everything*. Your financial, physical, social, emotional, everything. Look at every aspect of who you are and decide on what you want to recreate. You may not be able to recreate all of it at the same time, and the goal isn't necessarily to complete everything in one fell swoop. The goal here is to honestly see who you are and what you like and what you don't like and how you want to change those things you don't like. And be specific. If you are having social problems, ask yourself, "In what way am I suffering these social difficulties?" Be sure to state the specifics; you can begin to examine how to change those details into positives. If, in dealing with your social problems, you realize you feel awkward talking to new people or even getting out and meeting people, let that be your focus and then practice doing better. Practice when you're at home, with friends, looking in the mirror, practice your pitch, your introduction or greeting, and then you must get out and talk to people.

Step Three: Develop support for your journey. No man, or woman, is an island, so it's vital for your recreation to find guidance, prayer, and support. Make sure if you are a person of faith, you are praying over the things you're about to come across as you venture out into the world. Make sure you have a support system of at least one or two persons whom you can turn to when you're having doubts and be honest with them about what you're going to do. When you put that into motion while starting your self-assessment, write everything down. You'll want to see that list.

Step Four: Plan. You must plan what you're going to do and set realistic goals. When you travel, you prepare. When you do anything, you adjust. In planning, you must set goals. Let's take me for example. I knew I was going to leave teaching in 2016 after twenty years of working for the New York City Department of Education because I wanted to do something different with my life. So, I decided to return to grad school in January of that year. My goal was to get a degree in human services because I want to continue to help people in different ways. I also changed my writing because my future books are going to connect to the personal and business changes I've made. My goal for this second master's degree is writing the two curriculums or courses I have in mind for the direction I have planned once I finish grad school. Completing the next three books is another goal I have in mind. In July of 2016, I achieved one of my goals; I packed up my family and moved from New York to Delaware. After living in New York for over forty years, it was time to change this part of my life as well. I sat down and did the planning, I set the goals and time limits on when I wanted to achieve those goals, but it all started with the personal assessment. You must plan your finances the same way. With a strong understanding of how to make money, one knows it takes time and sound investments. Your planning efforts must include sound educational resources to assist you in your decision making. So, as you see planning covers all areas of your life if you want to reach the desired outcomes.

Step Five: Get to work. Step five is the step many people tend to fall short. It is simple but challenging: Get to Work. Plans and goals mean nothing if you're not looking to obtain them or achieve them. Get started because you cannot complete the race if you haven't started. The work won't always be easy, but with guidance, prayer, and support, the work *can* be accomplished. You need advice because once you put things in motion; you're going to need someone to remind you you've got this. If you are a person of faith, through the Bible, God, and Jesus, you'll receive support and love and guidance in a personal manner. On those days you are tired or are feeling doubtful, those who support you will sustain you, allowing you to get back on your feet and back into forwarding motion. We must use these things because when we are on this journey to the new us, there's going to be doubt, frustration, and failure because we're doing new things. You're now going to have to say to yourself, "How can I get through?"

What you can do to help you through these moments is create a snapshot of your recreation. What will it look like, feel like, and taste like when you complete the goal? Develop that picture and bury it in your mind, soul, and spirit, and hold fast to it on the days all seems for naught. On the days you want to quit, keep saying to yourself how beautiful the goal will be if you just push through this.

When you get to work, and you start working toward your goals, you're going to meet other people doing the same thing, and the networking and socializing will create opportunities for you to learn from others and to gain experience. You will see you are not alone. Are there going to be times when you are alone? Yes, but there were times when Jesus was alone; he said he needed to be alone. You must turn being by yourself into a positive. Take time alone to reignite your battery on what you need to do, to refocus yourself if the day didn't go the way you wanted. Become your internal cheerleader.

Step Six: Evaluate your progress. Now and then, stop and evaluate where you are. Are you ahead on what you planned on doing? Are you behind? Then, reevaluate the information. Once you do, you'll be able to make changes to your plan and actions for the next steps in the journey. Don't be discouraged if you are behind in your progress. We evaluate to return to stage four, looking at your plans. Maybe you made a mistake in planning, perhaps the goals you set were too lofty, so you need to reevaluate those plans but quickly get back to step five: get back to work. The recreation is not going to happen overnight; the new you are not going to show up overnight. You may have to go back and forth, but don't keep going back to step six because things aren't working out the way you want. Number six is another form of assessment. Am I putting in the energy? Am I focused? Remove the things which are distracting. Once I get to step six, and I don't like the progress I have made, my question should be "What is keeping me from the goals I set in step four?"

Step Seven: Push on to and through your goal. You got yourself in the race, you're pushing, and you can see the finish line. Many of us will ease up and let the fear of success pull us backward. After you've evaluated your progress and are back in the race; if now know what your goal is going to be, put your head down and push through the finish line. When you watch any race, you see the runners lean in to get to the finish line first. You see it in every sport. The closer competitors get to the finish line, the more you know it because the competitors are thinking of all the hard work which went into getting the job done. When you get closer to your goal, a part of you is going to want to shut down or ease up, but it is not over until you push all the way through.

So, in summary, here are the seven steps:
1. Get past the fear
2. Complete a self-assessment
3. Develop support for your journey
4. Plan
5. Get to work
6. Evaluate your progress
7. Push on to and through your goal

When looking at these steps, realize the process is recursive. Hardly ever does someone start at level one and cruise through to level seven. And that is okay. There will be trials and errors. There will be tweaks to the plans and goals. You will grow and perhaps even decide a goal you wanted to fulfill does not fit with who you are becoming. If you keep reassessing and moving forward and ultimately pushing *through* your goal, you will be more than fine.

The following are self-reflection questions to journal your thoughts or to sit and think about the content in this chapter. Give yourself a quiet space to read, think, and write on these matters. And be honest with yourself. Honesty and transparency is the key to you getting to your best self.

<u>Self-Reflection</u>

Bonding with Recreating Yourself

This chapter provides a 7-step process to recreate yourself. It's important to note the process is recursive; you may find yourself in step 3, for example, and having to cycle back to step 1 before moving forward. It's not a race to the finish line. There's only one person in your race: you.

1. Get past the fear. What fears, worries and doubts are keeping you from fulfilling a goal? How can you get past those fears? What mantras can you create? What daily rituals can you perform to kill fear?

2. Complete a self-assessment. Think about all facets of you: mental, emotional, physical, spiritual, financial, social, etc. What aspects need development? What kind of growth does each side need?

3. Develop support for your journey. This journey can be treacherous. Because of this, you must have a reliable support system in place to motivate you and help to push you forward. Who can you turn to for guidance, prayer, and support? How can you offer these things to yourself?

4. Plan. What is the goal you plan to achieve? What are realistic mini-goals you can reach to make it to the finish line?

5. Get to work. You have a goal. You have a plan to achieve the goal. The only thing left is to do is the work.

6. Evaluate your progress. This is where the recursive process may appear. As you examine what you've done and compare it to your plan and your goal, you may find the need to cycle back to previous steps to fine-tune your strategy and purpose. Ask yourself: what successes have you had in your pursuit? What failures have you had? Has your approach changed since the start of your quest? If there were changes,

OUR BOND IS OUR GIFT

figure out how they affect your strategy. If there were no changes, then ask yourself what you might need to do differently going forward to eliminate failures and increase successes.

The Power of Life and Death in a Word

Not too long ago, I realized something: your whole life can be turned upside down on the words of another person.

I had to go to family court to answer to allegations made by a family member. In talking to a person involved with social services, she explained the claims being made against me and I grew angry. None of it was real, and I was wondering why my family member would place me in a lie of this magnitude.

I will admit. Initially, I was letting my emotions get the best of me the more I thought about these allegations. My wife reminded me things would grow worse if I don't check myself. I eventually returned to myself because I knew had the truth on my side. I told myself I needed to lean on that truth and trust the Lord will see me through this mess.

When I went to court, I kept myself calm, and I explained everything to the court-appointed lawyers assigned to my case. Again, I reminded myself to remain calm as I was giving them the insight on who I was and truth of what was going on here. In doing so, once we were able to see the judge and offer the information about this case and showing proof to the lies told, they realized all the information they were given from my family member was erroneous. At that moment, something struck my spirit; even though I was happy they were able to figure out my situation, I wondered: what would have happened to someone who wasn't able to calm themselves as I did? What happens if it's a younger gentleman or somebody else who gets so angry about the lie being told about them they act out of character, giving this flawed system, which is messing up lives, more reasons to continue the chaos in their life?

Once on Facebook, I started the Lord picks you to carry the burden of some substantial things, and in remembering, I knew I was chosen for a reason. I was, and still am, built for stuff like what happened to me. I'm not bragging or boasting when I say this. I've learned over the years my talents are a high patience level, a high tolerance for B.S. as they say. Part of it was groomed from teaching for 20 years under challenging schools in tough urban neighborhoods of Brooklyn, New York. Another portion comes from being a Christian and growing in my understanding of the role faith plays in our lives. I've come to learn and pay attention to how people act. And in knowing that, I can develop myself to withstand the negativity which might come my way.

During my legal woes, one negative thing which came my way was the lawyer assigned to me. She wouldn't listen to me; she had her idea of what needed to be done, but I couldn't go with her agenda. Amid this storm, I still *knew the* truth, and I made sure she knew she was working for me and I needed her to tell the court what I had to say. Sure enough, as they began to go over all the information, they realized nothing they had was factual. I should have been happy, but I was still bothered because everyone in the courtroom was smiling except the person who had been done dirty: me. No one wanted to consider what I was dealing with, and it made me think about people who can't afford a defense. People are given public defenders who may not have the time, energy, or concern to deal with their clients appropriately. As a result, their clients will grow frustrated, not knowing what to do, and will walk into the courtroom and accept anything.

Although the situation bothered me, I had to close my eyes and pray and thank the Lord for allowing me to get through it and for allowing me to see the inner workings of this space because I had a better understanding now of how to deal with other people. I already had an excellent knowledge of how family court worked because this situation made the seventh time I was there... with no negative effects.

I realized the importance of remaining calm when in tight predicaments. I had to stay respectful and be knowledgeable about the proceedings. I had to have my paperwork laid out in a way which was understandable to those who spoke on my behalf. I had to release my anger and begin and understanding this system is a process. If you ever have to go through this process, there will be moments of frustration and anger, but by pushing through those moments, you will make it to the finish line.

I mentioned this above, and it bears repeating: prayer works. The first thing I did, and I would suggest others do, too, was pray because in doing so we humble ourselves to God. And when we do, we are placed in a better position, a position that knows if God has our backs, if we see God is protecting us, then we do not need to worry. Our goal is to keep moving forward and doing what we can. We must walk with a confidence which comes from our belief in God. We must be mindful of what we say and to keep negative thoughts and comments from our minds and mouths. We must listen more than we speak, we must make sure we think before each word comes from our mouth because people are not just looking to your words; they are watching your actions with your words. What this means is even if you're angry, you can't sit with a mean look on your face and have a dangerous position if you want things to go your way. We need to have a humbling place, which I know is difficult to have when you're angry. Make people wonder why you are so calm amidst your storm. While they question, how do you remain composed, you will know you're leaning on a

OUR BOND IS OUR GIFT

God who has you in this state of peace which indeed does surpass all understanding.

This doesn't mean you can't have moments of anger or you can't cry if you're upset. Many of us are under the impression tears are a sign of weakness. They are not, and I learned a long time ago. Tears reflect our feelings, and if we feel strongly about something, of course, emotion is going to come, so tears are going to happen.

With my situation in family court, I kept my emotions in check, and through my calm demeanor, everyone – from the judges, the lawyers the court assigned to me, to the lawyers on the other side – saw what the truth was, and they also saw me in a different light.

My story could have ended negatively. God knows I have experienced and have seen many situations in which people faced dire straits. But here's the truth: if you have God in your life, you have everything you need. They may take time from you, material, even money because you must spend money to defend yourself. Understand this: God can, and often will replace all which has been taken away.

The story I've been telling you illustrates this perfectly.

How so?

During this same time of the court case, I was preparing for my move to Delaware; I took three days off to make a job interview and to look for houses. I wasn't supposed to get paid for the third day because I only could use two personal days. At the time, I didn't care about the money lost. These were things I *needed* to do.

On the third day, I had to go to court, and because I went and had the court documentation to prove I was there, I was paid for the day. Not only did God allow me to walk out of the courtroom with no charges and a bunch of "I'm sorry for wasting your time, Mr. Belvin,", I also was paid from my job for having to be there, so the Lord made sure I got paid for my problems. The minute a blessing like this comes to you, it's important to thank God and keep it moving. Do not boast or gloat. Do not be arrogant or disrespectful to anyone. Do not throw your victory into the face of others. Just be humble

It's the same with anger. Do not keep the hostility you have toward the people who caused you strife. Pray to God they find the help they need to deal with the lies said. For me I was prepared if things had gotten worse, I had my wife and the Lord with me. I would have dealt with the outcome and continued to deal with the situation. We both would have fought and kept fighting until the truth was known.

Not everyone who reads this will be of the Christian faith, but if I'm going to walk in my truth, so I have to say this: when you go through a negative experience, you must learn to trust the people who the Lord places in your life. As well as trusting the fact the Lord will see you through any situation you are dealing with. Now I know this may not sit well with everyone who reads it, but you must lean on what gets you through your tough times as I did by replacing the Lord with whatever works for you. However, for me and mine, we choose the Lord.

The scripture sometimes shows a brother can turn on a brother because one wants what the other has. The story is not a new one. In fact, most of us have either witnessed it or been told a story about a person who harmed a dear friend or family member out of jealousy and greed. Although the story is not new, you can't allow yourself to live this way if you can avoid it. We must work hard not to get so caught up in personal greed, and our wants to such a degree we would harm another to obtain the possession sought. God has plans laid out for us. And if those ideas are in place, we need to accept things will happen whether we want them to or not. After we decide to

OUR BOND IS OUR GIFT

admit, we then need to ask this question: how am I going to handle the situation?

There is an interesting saying: It is cool to be a Christian until the devil shows up. Some of us have no idea how to deal with evil placed in front of us. However, if we came in believing God, then we must go out believing in God. And if we think we can learn to accept circumstances, we can deal with the situations which occur.

Sometimes, you need to close your mouth and let God work, but too often we forget about the power of life and death in our mouth. Too often, we want the whole world to feel what we feel when all we should do is just shut up and let God work. God sees the same things, you know, and of course, he already knew what was going to happen. If God is for your good, and he knows what's going to happen, then we can assume he will give us a way out. We don't need to have perfect clarity in a situation to resolve it. We don't have to bemoan our circumstances to solve them. Often, we just need to tiptoe away from the evil of a position. Sometimes, it's okay to just ease past the devil, to walk past silently without saying a word. You don't want to engage him; you just want to get away from him. God will deal with him, but when you sit there screaming, you might get something you don't want: a war you might not be able to win. Many lives were lost fighting conflicts they were not supposed to fight, and sometimes God covers us for a reason and moves us on without you saying a word for a reason. We want the world to know we are hurting, but there are times when we just need to say a thank you and move on or drop to our knees to pray for those who might harm us.

When I was forced to go to court, I—with God's help— could rise above any anger I had and to present myself positively to bring the proper information to the table and not to get angry about why I was being made to go on this journey.

My positive presence, my positive actions, and words gave people pause. Some gave me a look as if to say, "Isn't he the one being brought up on foolishness? How is he so calm?"

Well, I showed them, God. I showed them the reflection of a faith in God which emits from me. Too many of us do not know what it means to reflect the God we claim has our faith. We talk a great game, a fantastic game, but it is easy to tell when you're holding two aces in poker. Try to talk the talk with two threes in a poker game. See if you can make money with two threes. It's not as easy. You must understand the power of life and death is in what you say, but you should also comprehend who granted you the strength. You must also recognize what power can do when channeled the right way. They say once you ring a bell you cannot undo the ringing, and this applies to relationships and the communication within those relationships. When we say hurtful things, to ourselves or others, those words cannot be erased. We must think before we speak. We must be careful what we talk about within our relationships with our significant others, our children, our bosses, our coworkers, etc.

And most importantly, be careful what you say about yourself. Your word has value. It can lift you up or tarnish your reputation. In court, I was determined to show the judge I was a person of worth and meant I had to make sure my lawyer defended me in the best way possible. The lawyer given to me worked *for* me. My lawyer, like any lawyer, made suggestions and told me what I should do based on her professional opinion, but this didn't mean I didn't have my questions and suggestions.

At one point during the case, the lies about me were offered. I asked the lawyer, "Aren't you going to explain to the judge this information is incorrect? Aren't we going to explain

OUR BOND IS OUR GIFT

they have my name wrong? Aren't we going to say to the judge I wasn't there? I was not connected to this."

"Well, it is a preliminary hearing," she replied. "I will see what I can do."

No, I thought, *what do you mean you will see what you can do? You're going to say this, or I'll say it my damn self.*

If you're going to work with me, then you are going to go as hard as I go. If I'm going to lose at anything, if my character, credibility, and anything which has to do with who I am as a man are going to be questioned. I will be damned if I'm not going to step up and speak for myself when I know I am a child of God. There is no way I am going to sit there and not allow myself to be heard when I serve a God who demands I be who I am supposed to be. I am not supposed to hide from him or anybody, so am I going to sit quietly and allow myself to be done dirty? Never! That's not in the scriptures I read and has nothing to do with the God I pray to, the Jesus I follow.

Looking back at the morning of the hearing, I got up at 6:50 a.m., went to my office, and prayed, "Lord, whatever it's going to be, it's going to be, but I'm not going to go out quietly."

And I meant it.

I was not going to let anyone lie about me and not have an opportunity to say something. I love God too much not to speak my truth. Even during the hard times. God said it wasn't going to be easy, and if I was going to follow him, then I couldn't get upset when things, in fact, got tough. What I had to do, and I am suggesting **you** need to do, is thank him. Thank him for telling you ahead of time things would get rough. Thank him for building you to withstand the turbulent times.

Like I wrote earlier, it's easy to be a Christian when there is nothing on the table. When you don't risk anything, you get to sit in the confines of your home and your church and yell and scream and jump loudly for the Lord. And that's fine, but can you do these things when the tables turn, and your life gets ripped apart at the seams? Can you praise and worship when people call you out your name because of hearsay? Can you honor and pray when you have nothing left?

It is vital for you to be able to reach that point in your life. In the very center of the hurricane, you need to hold your head high; have a stiff, straighten back; and speak your truth to anyone who will listen. You need to keep your peace and not let anger for people who have wronged you infiltrate your space of peace. Remember, people are just doing their jobs. In dealing with the court case, I was not angry with those who were prosecuting or the judge. They were doing their jobs. And I had a job to do, too. lucky for me, I have a boss who is more significant than all other bosses.

And I have a boss who is big on sharing with me. I can speak positively about my life and my circumstances because I take time to spend time with God.

When you take time to sit quietly and allow everything going on around you to be pushed out, and you listen to what is inside you, you will hear God because it will be the voice of reason amidst all the tribulation going on inside you. It will be the thing which calls out to what you should do when all this confusion is going on inside you. If you don't understand what the Holy Spirit is, then nothing I'm saying is going to make sense. God gave you a piece of himself to put inside you so you could speak to your father directly—with your words or with your heart. Close the noise out from around you, move away from your friends and family for a little while if you must, and go somewhere private. My grandmother would lock herself in her kitchen and have her moment with God. You must give yourself time for God to speak to you, and you do this by sitting still, being quiet, and listening. In listening, positivity will start

OUR BOND IS OUR GIFT

to emerge from your soul. Some call it 'the conscience,' but it's God.

You stop and listen, and you will hear things like, "You shouldn't have done this" and "Therefore, you should go here."

God does not want his children lost, and if you're tired of being lost, then you need to acknowledge who God is so he can speak to you. Acknowledging God doesn't prevent bad times. We all will have bad times. We might suffer losses as well, but when we have God, and we know we have him, nothing is ever indeed lost.

As a Christian, you will face the devil. You'll have opportunities to tiptoe past him and keep moving forward quietly, and you'll have moments when you need to stand toe-to-toe with the devil and speak down every lie he tries to get you to believe. He'll whisper your fears and doubts and worries and anxieties. He'll try to make you question every good thing you know and have experienced.

But you have the WORD of the Bible. The word of God and the words from your mouth to crush the devil's lies, speak the moral truth, and allow God to make ways out of no means.

Learn the word of God. Apply the word now and always.

Below are self-reflection questions to journal your thoughts or to sit and think about the content in this chapter. Give yourself a quiet space to read, think, and write on these matters. And be honest with yourself. Honesty and transparency is the key to you getting to your best self.

<u>Self-Reflection</u>

Bonding with the Word

"But let your 'Yes' be 'Yes,' and your 'No,' 'No.' For whatever is more than   these is the evil one." –Matthew 5:37

Our words matter. The words we say to ourselves, the words we speak to others, and the words we take in from external sources.
Much like in the chapter on bad communication, you should reflect on how your words are used to help (and hurt) you on your journey.

1.   What words do you speak into your life? Do they fulfill and sustain you or crush you and your dreams? If you talk negativety into your life, what are the replacement words, phrases, sentences you can use to uplift yourself?

2.   What words do you speak into others' lives? Do they hurt and maintain the person or break them down and their ideas? If you talk negatively of others, reflect on why you choose that position. Are there hidden hurts or negative feelings which make you choose this path? How might you change the words you use to help and encourage others?

OUR BOND IS OUR GIFT

3. What words do others speak of your life? Do they fulfill and sustain you or defeat you and your dreams? If someone is talking negatively about your life, consider the source. Why might they be saying these things? Is there any truth to what they are saying? If there isn't, think how you might handle this situation differently. Do you confront them? Do you cut them loose? Do you provide yourself with replacement words to face the negativity?

Where's the Fruit? Judge a Tree by Its Fruit

How often do you listen to what someone says and instantly believe everything they say? You take their information and change the way you do things, change the way you think about situations.

Today, we don't have just our family and friends who will listen. We can go to millions of websites, view millions of videos, listen to millions of podcasts and live streams full of information. We're overloaded with content which infiltrate our consciousness.

In the chapter on bad communication, I mentioned my friend who teaches mass communication and how she teaches her students to critique the continuous stream of media which is a part of their daily life. Do we merely consume media and get sickeningly fat physically, emotionally and spiritually from it?

The same question can be asked of the people we keep in our lives. Are we merely consuming everything people tell us, or are we examining the fruits of those people we are listening to? Are we checking the credentials of those supplying the information? Are we being mindful of what we are allowing inside of us? Not every person who talks about your life is a notable professional. Not every person is trying to sell you a product that will help you.

For example, we can mention the products we sell like I suggest the books I write, the company I own, etc. If anyone wants to check me out, they can go to my blog www.keithBelvin.Blogspot.com and read about my experience, what I do, and decide to support me or not. I leave it up

OUR BOND IS OUR GIFT

to them. I always tell people to look at my site, my social media accounts, to Google my name because I think it is vital for everyone to coordinate the information to the credentials of those offering the insight.

It's easy for us to jump on the bandwagon and become a fan of the latest internet sensation, the person who says they can save your marriage and make you look great at the same time. But not checking out the person's credentials can leave you making tragic mistakes in your relationship, your life, and the lives of people you love.

The question which unsurprisingly arises is *how do I know if someone has my best interest in mind?*

Check the fruit (what's being offered to you). If a person is trying to help you, what they say will line up with useful information given from multiple sources. It will line up with news you have heard from other places. Let us keep it understood there is nothing new under the sun; there are different ways to go about doing very familiar things. I might have a unique spin on relationships, but I am still going to say excellent communication is a part of any stable relationship. And guess what? You will have heard the same statement from most people who speak on relationships. What makes that statement different from when others say it is how I use my personal experiences or my knowledge about relationships. I may, for example, tell you to do your research before you self-publish your book; this is not new advice. You are going to hear similar information and stories from other individuals. What may capture your attention with me may be where or how I did my research or the changes I made. You will notice the positive steps I decide for my life or the strides others have made will align if their path is in any way like my own. Consider when you're looking for a good workout regiment, for example. You will probably research people who are consistent with their workouts, athletes, or professional trainers. If you find some of the most well-known and influential athletes follow similar workout regiments and go to the same doctors, then you are more than likely to try those workouts because you believe they work. The same goes for those of you who are spiritually inclined. Not everyone with spiritual information to give have the credentials to provide information in meaningful ways.

Not too long ago, I was told to watch a Periscope video of someone who was giving wonderful money advice showing you how to make millions of dollars. On this social media platform, the person proclaimed themselves as a guru offering this advice via products to purchase. I did a simple Google search for the person because I figured this person's page would have tons of follow up. In searching, I found no new information about the person, their money-making opportunities, or how exactly they could help others. There were no real credentials to back up what the person was reporting to the world. Because I searched, I knew this to be a fake or scam. However, many were giving their money because they believed the spiel instead of seeking the truth.

When I give talks or live stream on social media, I do not come on and provide fraudulent information. Everything I talk about can be checked. When I give my website information, talk about my book, exchange about experiences all of it is verifiable. You can contact the New York City Department of Education, The New York State Education department, and you will see how long I have been teaching. My degrees have been confirmed from four different colleges. This is public knowledge. I was married and divorced; again, all general knowledge. I am transparent with my problems and solutions, so I do not have to hide from any of my information. My fruits are out there because I am about trying to help individuals and feel transparency helps with extreme clarity. But we must learn to help ourselves by gauging what and who we allow speaking into our minds, spirits, and souls. Do not be so drugged out by the numbers next to someone's name. Just because someone has 17-million followers does not mean the person has the information you need. Be careful. To be a part of anyone's movement, school, project, etc., you need to do the investigation to ensure the information provided is reasonable and proper for you. Do not allow someone's impassionate pitch and emotional plea to how they did what they did influence you because as Jay-Z said, what you eat does not make me; you know what happens in the bathroom.

It's also important to realize sometimes a person can't help you because their circumstance is part of that "right place, right time" phenomenon. They had a great idea and lightning struck. They can't explain the lightning strike. It doesn't mean their story is insignificant. Learning how they went about developing their idea is great but know the journey they took will probably not be the journey you take. If you take a quick look on the internet, you will see thousands of websites by people who ask you to give them money, so they can provide you with information on how to be successful. They will have testimonials, but they will also have a massive disclaimer which states there is no guarantee you will succeed like them. Well, how good is the information if I give you my money, but I don't become successful when I follow your lead? Even if people in your life have followed others and have found success, this does not guarantee you will. Each experience is different, and each person must gauge information and the information given to discern if the content is right for their life and goals.

You must do the investigating before you sit down and start pouring your heart out because you think this person is there for you. You must elevate yourself because you should be careful the person you are paying close attention to and trying to learn from may be learning from you and sizing you up. In the literary industry, I am a lone wolf. I do not have a sizeable literary group of friends. I am intimate with who I talk to about the personal and professional moves I make. I might see people, fellow authors, at different places, and we may talk on Facebook and things of that nature; however, I watch what I share. I do not like much of what I see in the literary industry as an independent author and publisher. I don't care about specific business practices. I don't knock another person's hustle; they are free to do what they choose. For me, I keep my distance, and I keep my head down and keep pushing toward the things I need to accomplish. I help people who need my help. I've found when assisting large numbers of people, some people don't need the assistance offered. They claim to need it so they can be close to you to watch and see what they can learn to use for themselves without providing credit. They don't want to pay for your help, but they want to be close enough to determine your expertise and apply it to their work. Learning this, I keep my professional fruit close the vest.

    Since 2007 when I came into this industry, I have always done adequate research. I research anyone who is doing something with books, and I see what the consistencies in specific areas are, so I can see what the industry norms are. I want to look at what the cultural and industry standards are and how do those standards work for me, and then I will do what I need to do for myself accordingly. But I noticed so many people would lean on others they believed had their best interest in mind when they didn't. Many of these people don't have a problem spending your money, but many do not want to hold the weight with you or will not promote you. They will pat you on your back and smile at you and tell you how much they like what you are doing. You never see a share or a mention of your book on their pages, you never have them shout you out on any of the promotional stuff they are doing on Periscope, Facebook, Twitter, etc. You begin to realize you are on your own. And to a degree, you are. You also must be careful of those people who want to come in and do business with you and then slide their name all over your work to the point you do not know whose book you are reading. I see people who publish other people and their name is larger than the authors. How is that?

Check the fruits.

Some people tell writers Amazon is the best to do publishing, but they don't explain to new authors the difficulty of making money if you go that route. They will just tell them this is the route they are supposed to take. If you don't check the fruit, then you will believe this information, and ultimately, you might lose a lot of money by not doing your homework and learning of other avenues.

Check the fruits.

As a teacher, I was always mindful of learning the source of information given to me. Even from fellow teachers. When another teacher approached with some papers she thought would help me in my work, I immediately asked what the content was, where did it come from, why would I use it. I asked questions. Some people became defensive, like *why would you question the information I give you*, and it's not my intention to offend. I intend to make sure everything I do and everything I use to do what I do is of the best quality.

And that means I am going to judge a tree by the fruit it bears. I am going to examine people who offer me things, and I am going to do that by considering who the person is, what the person does, and what have been the effects of the help they provide.

Look at the people who are speaking into your life. Do not allow them into your head, heart, and life without checking their background. The fruit they offer can cause you unforeseen problems, and once you accept this poison, it does damage to you, your family, or business. This type of injury is not always repairable. Therefore, you cannot be afraid to tell someone no and hit the stop or end button on what they have placed in your life already. Do not be scared because, in the end, you are responsible for the choices you make for you and your loved ones. Do not blame someone if the fruit is poisonous unless they forced it on you.

Poisonous fruit comes wrapped in beautiful packaging, but you must take a more in-depth look at what you're being offered and from whom. Merely put, think of Eve, she allowed the snake to talk her into sampling fruit she already knew would cause significant problems. Don't let this to be your fate.

The following are self-reflection questions to journal your thoughts or to sit and think about the content in this chapter. Give yourself a quiet space to read, think, and write on these matters. And be honest with yourself. Honesty and transparency is the key to you getting to your best self.

Self-Reflection

Bonding with the Fruit

As has been mentioned in the chapters on bad communication and the life and death in the word, it is important to examine who provides "the word," the content, the information we consume. This reflection is more about what you can do to

monitor others' (and your own) communication and determine whether the fruits are worth taking in.
It might be difficult to do this when in the heat of verbal exchanges, but you should be thinking about.

1. What the person is saying?

2. What is the person trying to show?

3. How does what the person is saying connect to who the person shows you they are on a regular basis. Is there a variance?

4. What contextual information about the person is displayed and what positively or negatively influences are revealed?

    If someone who has been married four times, has cheated during each of those marriages, and is currently alone is attempting to give you sound marriage advice, then you want to think about 1, 2, and three above.
The fruit may not be bad coming from this person. If she has learned from her past, has changed for the better, and is using her mistakes to teach positive lessons, then her advice might be helpful.
    If she hasn't learned one thing, continues to make mistakes, and wants to play relationship guru, then you might consider "hearing" her advice, but not "listening" and allowing it to enter you as truth.

Fixing Men to Heal Their Relationships

I believe men need to get in a place in their lives in which they can then look to connect with women who are going to enhance them and whom they will equally strengthen.

Sadly, so many men were not taught how to act from their family, and they do not have a connection to God to help them. They walk through their lives with a defensive posture, taking women and using them. They do not know how to connect to each other, and they do not understand support and protection come from being connected to each other.

As men, we have this belief we must do it all alone, but we can't. No one can. Men must reach out to other men and acknowledge their greatness. Just as women need the support of other women, men need the assistance of other men. Once they recognize their importance, they then should prove greatness through their renewed behavior and actions. Another thing we can learn from men is how to treat women and how to connect our lives with good women to create good unions.

Men, like women, need to be capable communicators. Women are not minded readers, no matter how often they seem able to read our minds. Your significant other will not know what she can do to help you achieve more significant, better things unless you speak up. Although you may not have been taught how to express yourself, or how to openly allow your emotions to be seen, you can train yourself *how*.

Yes, many of us have been taught our emotions are weaknesses. Crying is for females. Man up. Dust it off your shoulders. I say this all the time: tears are not weaknesses;

they are reactions to emotions. I love my wife and my child, and the thought of something happening to either one of them or any of my children is going to bring emotion, which is going to cause tears. Does this make me weak? Not at all, but I must be comfortable with me to be able to show my emotions and be okay with it. When I can express myself freely, my wife gets the full me, which makes it easier for me to lead our relationship—and to have her take the lead when her gifts require her to be outfront. I must humble myself and know she got this. I often humble myself and sit and listen to my children because there may be things they are connected to I may not understand initially. There is nothing wrong with being sensitive. I am a sensitive dude, and I put it in my writing, but my sensitivity does not take away from my masculinity.

I express myself in my writing and when I talk to others, and primarily when I teach it's in an expressive way. I have conditioned myself to be expressive because I know the children I educate, my wife, and the people I meet at my speaking engagements need to hear and feel what I am saying. They need to see the emotions connected to what I am saying. Without feelings, I just present words, and we all have heard the saying, *actions speak louder than words*.

I believe our ability to accept our sensitivity starts with our Godly connection. Then, when we have ourselves right with God, we turn and choose the woman who reflects the values and beliefs we have so when we are together, we have a commonality we can build on. If you are not a believer in God, a lot of people are not, I do not have a problem with that choice. You still should find a significant other who has the synchronization you do so together you'll have a strong foundation to build upon. Your children, if you have them, will be blessed from the commonality.

K.L. BELVIN

One thing the scriptures show us is women is men's equal. We might not have the same physicality, but we are both, men and women, emotional, spiritual, and every other aspect. We need to appreciate this truth and abide by it. This is our first real commonality. This commonality bridges us. What differentiates us are aspects we should marvel in, give thanks for. When you watch a woman when she is nurturing a child, for example, you should marvel at the way the child and mother interact. I love watching my little girl and my wife communicate because it's unique to them. I have the daddy-daughter thing, and I adore it, but I like what my daughter and wife build between them. My wife and I, in our partnership as parents, celebrate the individual relationships we build with our daughter, and we are confident enough within our marriage to know when we need to be a certain way for our daughter. For example, there are times when I might have to be the disciplinarian and my wife the nurturer, and there are times when those roles are reversed. Because we want the best for our family, we do whatever needs to be done.

Unfortunately, some men believe women tend to the kids, more than them. These are the same men who will wonder why their kids have wandered into the treacherous terrains of life as they grow older but never reach back to be their father. Children need to interact with their fathers. They need to hear "I love you," they need the cuddles, they require you to play with them, whisper jokes in their ears, rub noses, tell stories, give advice—all things that aid them in becoming good young men and women. We should learn how to be open. It should come naturally, but because of all the outside influences which affect behavior and speech, we have drifted so far away from what the family could look like because we are shaping it on how society and media tell us families should look like, and we must get away from that. We have to get back to looking at and considering what the family unit can be and the power in that.

There was a time, primarily as folks of color, when the family unit sustained us during some very nasty and negative moments in this country's history and our history. Although we do not deal with travesties like those from our past now, we are still in the same mentality with other things. In many of our communities, because of economic situations, we are still in a type of bondage, but to overcome this, we must look at each other, our wives, husbands, and children and say we must close our doors and fix what is wrong, protect each other. For example, instead of buying $200 shoes, we could buy the $60 or $100 pair and take the saved money and invest it into our infrastructures, so our foundations are not controlled by those who do not share the same color. We must start teaching our children the truth and not the fictionalized history which has been shown or given to us.

The negative behaviors have kept some men unable to sustain good relationships with women and/or their children; those practices must end.

Think about those who suffer from drug addiction. In trying to break this habit, the addict will need to cut the use of the drug first, heal from the need of that medication, figure out what his life is going to be without drugs, and move into a new life—and continue to affirm why this is the best decision to make.

Many men think they need multiple women for their life to be complete. As an "addict" to this line of thinking, these men would have to feel like the drug addict who desires to be free. They would first need to remove themselves from this line of thinking. They would need to recognize they don't need a lot of women. They would need to be strong enough to delve into their lives to figure out where this line of thinking came from so they can heal themselves from it. They would need to visualize their life free of multiple women. They would need to enjoy life with their *one* real woman. If variety is what a man needs, then he doesn't need numerous women for that; he can have a conversation with the woman he is with and spice up the relationship any way they wish within the confines of their home. These men would seek the word of God and talk with men who are in stable, long-lasting relationships to glean knowledge from them. They would apply that knowledge to their relationship. And most importantly, as they would work on themselves and their relationship, they would be very mindful of their children.

They should become your priority. The last thing you want to do is create an environment for your child which fosters terrible behaviors, values, and beliefs about themselves, the opposite sex, and relationships. In doing so, they will go out into society and perpetuate the same foolishness you are doing because they do not have the guidance necessary to succeed in their walk-in life.

When you come to a place of balance in your life, your job is not finished.

No.

You must reach one and teach one.

You go out and find other brothers and help them. You cannot keep this information to yourself; you cannot keep your success and knowledge to yourself. You must go out and find other brothers who are lost and bring them to the light. If you think sitting there with your successes is the way it is supposed to be, then you are foolish. Many men come up with a lot of weak excuses about why they cheat, but here's one reason they will probably be too embarrassed to share: something is missing in them. They shouldn't be ashamed. Most of us have something missing from us. Those who admit this problem and then work to fix the problem are the ones who will succeed. This emptiness, this missing part either was put there because these men do not have a connection to their father, or they do not understand what being a real man is. They have been connected to so many external forces which do not talk about being real men, so they go out and destroy themselves because of the emptiness. A real man looks inwardly. He looks at what is missing and fixes it. Then he looks for a partner who is also focused because he knows together the two of them can become a force which is going to be very difficult to topple. Look at all the relationships you think are tremendously positive. They are successful because as a unit, the couple does not believe the world can do anything to them.

Maturity breeds confidence. When you can speak your truth, and find a mate whose truth matches yours, personal growth is inevitable. That growth is your maturity, and that maturity shows itself in the confidence you have not only in your relationship but also in your desire to see others in positive relationships. To obtain this, we men need to connect ourselves to God, ground ourselves in God, and search for women who are going to be equal partners. Together, you two should start looking to heal others around you in whatever form works for you to do so.

And in helping others, you should keep close to you this fact: not everyone will want your help, and it's okay.

It's been seventeen years since my ex and I parted ways.

And she's still upset.

Why, because I am happy? I went on to more without her than I was with her.

I am an excellent father to my sons despite her trying to say and prove otherwise.

Every way she has tried to bring me down has failed, yet she is still irritated. Maybe my ignoring her feelings towards my successes is why she holds on to her angry.

I pray for her. I do not say anything. I stay dead quiet. When I go to the house, I do not even go to the door. I tell the boys to come outside, and we go where we must go.

I am not going to add to someone's dismay. My job in life is to try to heal people's pain. Rule number one: if you throw a life preserver out to someone in the water, and they throw it back with anger, you do not throw it back. You just find someone else to save.

Even God did not save everyone.

The one person, however, we must fight to save is the boy child, for he is forgotten. The family structure is so fragmented the boy child loses out because he does not have proper guidance. If I asked you to put a puzzle together and gave you all the pieces of the problem, most of us would look back at the box to see what the completed mystery looks like to understand where the puzzle pieces go. But if I take away the cover, you might eventually finish the puzzle, but depending on how many parts are in it, most of us would quit because it becomes too complicated. This is what can happen to our young men because they don't have finished products, real men, to show them what they are supposed to do. Without the finished product, the road becomes treacherous. Most children because they have not been taught resolve quit. When the male child quits, he then looks for something else to play with, and most of the time what he chooses is something detrimental to himself and everyone around him. Sadly, most men who leave their families stranded do not realize they are removing the puzzle box, so there is no example, and the mother will do what she can. But when she is standing there trying to be an example as a mom, you should be careful because the child then projects himself to what he gets from the mother, which can explain why we have so many young men who have taken on feminine qualities and their masculinity has declined.

I can only tell you what I see in schools, young men who do not know how to react to males in authority. In the last school where I taught, there were over one-thousand kids and only two male teachers, one Caucasian man and myself. How these young men from kindergarten to fifth grade are supposed to grow into the well-rounded men, they should be when at an early impressionable age, there are no definite examples (or too few examples) to learn from?

Sadly, these young boys move on to junior high school and start getting in trouble when they finally must deal with male teachers. When they do, you hear the same things from their parents: "I do not understand what has gotten into him. He was never like this before." And it's true; he was never like this before. But think about where he came from, a place with two male teachers, and look at where he is now: an area with many male teachers, strong male teachers, some of them who exact firm discipline. Because these young boys had not been exposed to continuous male connections, he now does not know how to deal with the regulations from a male with firm rules. No person can be without rules and regulations for years and immediately change when presented with them.

My mission is to get older brothers to come back home and fix these relationships they destroyed. Television and modern society tell us to discard our current association and start a new one. We have abandoned relations and left our women alone with our children. We have decided our former woman and children are not important, so we'll start a family over here and not go back and heal the family we started over there.

You cannot do that.

One of the things I have realized in dealing with family court and dealing with the young men in family court situations is the system we have in place was not designed to deal with men who have multiple babies all over the place because that is not the way family was perceived. We are destroying ourselves by at least not going out and trying to explain to older and younger men they cannot keep creating these families they cannot take care of because the damage to the future is almost impossible to eradicate. We must start holding the people in our immediate circles to harder, higher standards. We need to tell our people the energy and work required to love one woman is more than enough. It's unfortunate it has become almost a badge of honor to be the player. I was that player, and it is the reason I wrote *From Gigolo to Jesus*. Growing up, older men encouraged me to be disrespectful to women because they said it was how I would get the credit I needed. They cheered me when I was with various women and did different sexual things. Sex had become my focus instead of me growing as a man. It took me destroying me and many lives along the way to realize how I was living was not how I *should* have been living.

Once you become a "good man," there are still plenty of troubles which can arise. One comes from understanding the daily lives of good women.

Every day, at the bus stop, laundromat, daycare pickups, and on and on, thirsty dudes, men whose sole purpose is to use women, are at the ready with sweet words and big smiles, waiting to lure a woman into their selfish traps. Women hear this foolishness so often that when a good man like you comes around and offers a simple comment like "I like your hair," many women do not know how to react. It's not they are disrespectful, its no good dudes have created in these women

OUR BOND IS OUR GIFT

an automatic defense. As men, we must understand our eager counterparts are out there, and we must offer to heal our sisters without making our words and actions something sexual or some conquest. Do not get offended if you provide a positive word and the woman does not respond. Continue to be a good man; continue to offer positive words, to listen. In time, defenses will dissolve, and when she sees you, she'll think, *every time I see that dude he is saying something beautiful to me and does not want anything*. She will respond to you because ultimately, she will know inside, you're right.

How you first act when trying to connect with her is exactly how you should continue to interact with her. Don't be the man who sweet talks and does the romantic gestures to get her only to drop all the love things when you "got" her. Continue to talk to her, and most importantly, continue to listen. Be truthful, transparent, and provide her with a safe space to be those things to you, too.

Unfortunately, too many brothers are taught conquest, and too many sisters are taught defend against the conquest. Everyone is in a defensive posture like the prelude to the war, and now we are just waiting for someone to make a mistake so we can have an all-out showdown. Someone must be a peacemaker, the light for a change. Someone must sit down with our sisters and say, "I do not want anything from you but to see you better and healed." And then we should offer this same sentiment to the men.

Understand this may be more difficult to do with men than with women. Most men have been taught not to show emotions, so their defenses go up when you begin asking them to share their feelings. It can be even harder when a man tries to educate another man. If you see a man talking ignorantly to a woman if you walk up to him and say, "Can I holler at you for a second? The way you spoke to the sister was very disrespectful," don't be surprised if his testosterone levels rise and he takes offense to you butting in. You must be careful not to let anger rear its ugly head on your side of the conversation. Find a mutual connection, some way to find common ground so when you offer your advice, the man will listen.

None of us like confrontation, but it is essential for us all to be healers, to reach out to teach and comfort, even if it seems daunting. It hurts me to see a woman burdened, in pain and I know someone like the old me caused that. Because God brought me out of my past, I owe him, and the only way I can pay God back is to try to heal as many people who are being damaged by the man I used to be. And it doesn't matter if you have had a dark past or not; we all should work to heal our men, and our women so strong unions can be formed, unions which positively affect not only the man and woman in the union but also the children produced through the union.

We must commit ourselves to the changes we want to see. Gandhi said be the change you want to look at, and we should be that. As men, it is our responsibility to try to heal within us the damage done by other women because if we do not fix it, it is only going to come back to affect us in some way, whether with our daughters, sisters, mothers, and wives. As men, we must take the lead to be able to show women not all of us are what many of us appear to be. We must make sure we are grounded in the Lord, and we do not make our actions and words about vanity. When I was running the streets, I understood pain, so I manipulated suffering to get what I wanted. I made the illness appear to be fixable when dealing with me because I was different from those someone else has dealt with. I had no desire to heal; I was all about conquest. Conquest as a man should be replaced with healing, but you must humble yourself first to understand you are a servant to others, and it is your job to heal as many as you can through

OUR BOND IS OUR GIFT

the Godly actions you give to this world. If you are in church every Sunday, God bless you, but who are you on the other six days of the week? Do they understand the God in you to be able to help them release the pain in them? Because this is the only way to do it, you must give people reason to release their pain. Why would someone who is fragile to being hurt come to you and open to you unless you have given them a reason to release pain? When they release it, you must heal it with something else. A hug is my way of taking my energy from my heart to help alleviate the lost power in your heart. A hug is real; it is a transfer of comfortable emotions to the one who is hurt and a way of saying, "I got you, and I do not want anything from you."

We have gotten to the point we are scared to hug, show true emotions or to counter the pain people are sufeering from with pysical contact. We must offer Godly passion and be light.

To my sisters, I apologize for men whom I do not know, men whom I do know, sons, boyfriends, fathers, husbands who got it wrong. Many of them got it wrong because they were never taught right, they know what they know. You might have thought they were different or believed they could have been different, but you cannot understand something you have never actually immersed yourself into. In going forward, one of your focuses when meeting a man is to talk about his past, family structure, and his road. He will look to dominate the conversation because he may not want you to understand some painful things about him but hold your ground and get him to understand some things about yourself because it is where you will start to see his truth. Yes, we must pray for healing, but we also must be the healing.

The vulnerability is the key. I am not saying stay with anyone who is negative. What I am saying is as their partner, you must get men to be able to discuss issues affecting them so better choices can be made in and around the relationship. I am not trying to say it's your job as the partners to heal men because you might not be able to help them and risk hurting yourself. However, there should be a conversation held because it is a form of protection for yourself. I feel much of the weight to help the men in crisis should come from their brothers. Because of testosterone, some men are not willing to let go of what they think is right. One thing I tell mothers about their sons is I can get further with their sons because as a male I can create a dynamic with their sons within a man-to-man conversation may not be found in a mom-to-son discussion. A young boy may be more likely to open up to a man than a female. This isn't to knock my sisters or the way they raise their children. However, what may be necessary to save the male child's life is something you might not be able to give. We must be able to work together to foster the healing needed.

While men are working on fixing themselves and women are working on helping men repair themselves, we *all* need to center attention to teaching our young folks the right ways to live in this society.

Our young folks are the missing commodity. Hitler once said, do not worry about their parents because I have their children. As evil as Hitler was, he was not an idiot. He was a brilliant man who did very evil things. Sometimes, we must look at the evil men do to understand how we can counter with positivity, but we also must listen when something is said which is formidable.

We must work with the children now. Even God said we must come to him as children. Children matter. Their wide-open love and trust should not be crushed so early in their development because of wayward parents and leave them to learn through society and media. We need to teach our children how to be good people, good boys, and girls, good young men and women, then good men and women so when they go out into the world, they are less likely to wreck themselves and others. Make sure the things your children consume – books, movies, videos, TV shows, games, etc. – foster positive images, values, beliefs, and attitudes. Make sure you spend time with your children and ask them questions and answer their questions. We need to allow our young boys to grow into the young men we know they can be and then help them, and then we need to get guidance from other men around us. We must help heal each other and find a way to raise our young princes to take our place as the future of your family name, so those coming after them know them only as kings.

The church has gotten a lot of things wrong, particularly regarding children. It says to raise a child up in what they should be, but we should not try to change who children are; we are supposed to enhance who they are. Too often, parents want children to become who they never became. In doing so, these parents are trying to change what God created. Allow your child to be what they are, enhance their gifts. It is opposite God when you try to change a child. My child likes to sing. Am I going to tell her to stop because it annoys me? No. If it annoys me, I'm still going to say, "Sing, doll" before I start singing with her. My wife likes to let our daughter dress, and in the end, she will have on one boot, a shirt, and panties. I always look at my wife as if to say, "Really, honey?" But our daughter is independent. I just smile and let her be her. Now, she is putting on her jacket, and she's not yet two years old. She's putting on her boots, trying to zip up my coat. We should allow children to find who they are in a safe environment.

You must pay attention to who your child is and give your child the opportunity to be who God created them to be. You are a steward, one who takes care of; you do not own your children and should not rule over your children. You should take care of them. God blessed you with the opportunity to care for your children; your job is to raise them up and eventually release them into the world to be who God made them be. If you interfere with this and cause a child to go in a different direction, then you need to see what the Lord says when you create a child to sin. The Lord says you should kill yourself, tie a millstone around your neck and throw yourself into the ocean, for there is no greater sin than taking a child in a different direction than where God created them to go. That is how you are supposed to use scripture, not beat each other over the head with it. We are supposed to show how scripture applies to real life. Provoke children not to wrath because it is in those moments children will do things which are not smart. As parents, we are not supposed to push our children into angry situations where they do things out of stupidity because they do not have the knowledge or control of the anger you caused. That does not mean your children are always going to like you. It does not mean you'll become your children's best friend either because discipline is going to come in the form of chaffing, which the child may not like. You cannot just do things you know are wrong for your child because it is right to you.

    To help repair men and fix their relationship problems, a well-rounded approach must be adopted. We must look at the connection young men have with older males and their influences. Then we must remove those variables which prevent them from becoming the loving partners God intended to be. This may be a more significant social issue I am sure, but we can attempt to fix the things within our circles. If enough put in the energy, men will slowly start to become what we envision them to be: outstanding sons, leaders, fathers, and significant husbands.

The following are self-reflection questions to journal your thoughts or to sit and think about the content in this chapter. Give yourself a quiet space to read, think, and write on these matters. And be honest with yourself. Honesty and transparency is the key to you getting to your best self.

Self-Reflection

Bonding with Healing Men

So many men need to be healed so they, in turn, can improve their relationships. Hopefully, by this point in the book, you have thought about what transparency means to you, what words uplift and dismantle you and others, and more. And from those things, you have begun to think about the areas in your life which need to be healed.

  1. The past. Current behaviors often derive from past actions. Think about romance, love, relationships, marriage, family, "being a man." Where did you learn the concept of and meaning of these words? What visuals did you have to illustrate these words? What positive memories do you have when you think about these words? What negative memories do you have?

  2. The present. What past teachings are present in how you currently think about romance, love, relationships, "being a man"? Are there any past teachings which have hindered your ability to sustain a stable relationship?

3. The future. How can you modify and/or eliminate previous lessons so that you have a positive frame of reference for these words?

OUR BOND IS OUR GIFT

Why Are Our Young Men Angry?

As a twenty-plus-year educator and mentor who has started young men groups in Brooklyn, I realize to answer the title question, we must look at the totality of a person's life.

We must bring individuals who represent that life to the table. We need to bring folks who serve the single mothers, people who are trying to reach fathers who are absent, community leaders who are trying to work on local problems, educators, law enforcement, as well as the politicians to the table. Then we must sit down and hammer out what the future is going to look like and try to curb this steady decline of our young males' well-being. We are not having enough of that; we are too splintered to make substantial differences. We cannot ask why our young men of color are angry if we do not deal with the situation the single mother is in, what the schools are teaching or how they are attempting to reach our young men, etc. All facets of a life lived must be addressed because anger does not exist in a vacuum. It is an effect. Our goal is to find the causes and fix and heal and do better going forward.

Let the truth be known: our young men have a lot of reasons to be angry, and I think we forget that.

So, who should come to the table? Who do we talk to, talk with to get to the nucleus of this problem? There are at least six groups of people who should be involved in the conversation: the family, the church, the schools, the law, the politicians, and our communities.

The Family

First, we must talk to those within the family, the mothers, fathers, siblings. If there is an absentee father, despite the fantastic jobs done by many single mothers, the family unit is splintered. A young man needs to have someone to model his behaviors and choices after. If the father is out of the picture, there will be adverse effects on the young man.

But it's not just about having an absentee father; it's also about how the parents raise their children with good (or bad) beliefs, values, and attitudes. For example, some parents spoil their children, and those children grow up believing they are entitled to have the best because their parents gave them the best. When I see a kid wearing $300 jeans, $200 sneakers, $500 coat, and have a $500 phone on their hip, I am astonished. But this is not an anomaly. Not in 2017. Everywhere you look, you can spot a group of kids with the same expensive gear. When children see their parents fighting all the time, they see fighting as the norm. When children watch you treat other people like they are beneath them, they may grow up acting entitled and bullying others. Not too long ago, I spoke with Dr. Harper, a friend, and fellow author. She's a doctor and educator who specializes in the education of children and relationship counseling. She is currently a principal who has served hundreds of families and their children. She stated you would be amazed at how often we saw children as young as 3 or 4 years old with the mental makeup of adult type behaviors because children mimic what they see.

Many parents throw these expensive wares to their children to deflect from having to discuss the real problem.

I went through this with my ex-wife. She did not want to lose the love and affection of her kids when we were separated, pending divorce, so she would buy them things they did not deserve. It didn't matter to me; the actions made no sense. I could not control what she did, but I could manage what I did. When my boys were with me, they would get $60 for a pair of sneakers. They responded by saying, "Dad, we cannot buy anything with $60." But the truth was they couldn't buy what they **wanted** for $60, but they could buy a pair of sneakers. Apparently, my ex-wife had a problem with this because she would call and ask how were the kids going be able to buy sneakers with $60? She used money to tighten her connection with our children, but I wanted to teach them the value of it. We tell kids all the time not to worry about what someone else thinks, but then we do not arm them with how to deal with people's perceptions or explain to them what it's going to look like. Often it's because most of adults do not know how to deal with it either.

Parents should also be teaching children about the media, too. How we teach our children about the press is essential. Media thrives on negativity. So many people watch trashy reality TV shows where black men and women fight one another and curse and hate. Every night, the TV news begins its broadcast with the murders and crimes of the day. Sensationalism attracts people. Think about the accident on the highway and the rubbernecking which occurs because everyone's so nosey to see what happened. Media wants to connect to our basic wants and needs and desires—or create them for our children.

Instead of placing your children in front of technology and entertainment, take them outside. Once upon a time, play consisted of riding bikes and skateboards, playing dodgeball and kickball, and double dutch. If our kids don't know the value of actions outside of technology, which is our fault, the parents. Your children see what **to do** with you and your words and actions. If you say do one thing, yet personally you do a

OUR BOND IS OUR GIFT

whole different thing, your children will pick up on that and follow suit.

At two years old, my daughter was playing with her doll babies; she had them all lined up. She took a pamper and began to put it on one of her dolls. She took the baby, caressed her head, and said, "Lay down. Are you okay?" She was mimicking what my wife and I do for her; it was the most compassionate thing. It let me know the love we have for her is transferring to her wanting to share that love somewhere else. I am an outgoing and friendly person, so my daughter is an outgoing and loving person. Our children are the reflection of what we want to teach them; it is the transfer of love. But we cannot blame children when they do not get it. Most often, they do not get it because we are not presenting the correct things to them.

Many of our young men are angry because they are confused, and they are confused because we are confusing. Do you know how complicated it is to hear your mom say do well in school, and she cannot read? How confusing is it to have your parents give you a $500 cell phone without any parameters and then tell you to be responsible? How complicated is it to have your parents buy you a $2000 computer, place it in your room, and ask you to be accountable?

Psychologist B. F. Skinner talked about a system of consequences which are affected by rewards and punishments. If rewarded for negative behaviors, you would gravitate toward the adverse reaction. There is something to this. It is also Godly based. God says when you surround yourself with the wrong character of people it affects your style. It even affects your speech. If the Bible talks about it, and you have psychologists, you have science and religion talking about the same thing, there is something to pay attention to.

Who we surround ourselves with, what we surround ourselves with and allow to influence us affects how we speak and what we do.

Children know how to be responsible based on how we illustrate it to them. If we don't take time to understand the technology we give to our children, if we don't make the time to explain to them the good, bad, and downright ugly about the technology, then we are not equipping them with the knowledge they need to make informed decisions.

If you are not going to understand technology, then how do you expect to raise your children and make them viable in this world? When you cannot read a book, how dare you tell your child I want you to reach better heights, and you are not striving to be better. How do you explain to your daughter do not go out and get involved with this or that dude, yet you are not involved in a stable relationship? How do you tell your son, "Do not be like your father," but you do not talk to him about the type of man he should be?

The Church
As crazy as this may sound, the church can be a problematic entity when it comes to showing our young men the importance of having a healthy relationship with God.

Some older members often called older saints in African American churches are so stuck on religious rhetoric, they do not realize the attendance numbers of the church are declining. Young folks do not see Christianity as a viable option in their lives; often they go to church because they are forced to by their parents. One should never be forced to come to God; it should be an open offer to whoever, at whatever age they are. I am trying to work with progressive pastors and the progressive saints who understand, in their faith, God may be unchanging, but it doesn't mean the people attending church must do things the way their grandparents did. I am sure the horse and buggy were great during its time, but an air-conditioned car is a pleasant difference.

God is going to be who he is, who he said he is going to be. As a believer in the Christian faith, we believe times change. Jesus came to share with the holy men of the time that a change was needed. He wanted to bring light to how wrong their course of actions was in those days. His focus was to the church members of that time. Jesus wanted to show the Ten Commandments were legitimate laws and unchanging. However, he was going to show everyone how to follow the rules, while reducing things to two standards which were (1) loves God with all your heart and (2) love your neighbor the same way you love God. If you do those two things, you will keep to the Ten Commandments. He came and gave us a cheat sheet. During his time on the earth, Jesus showed the world things must be done differently. Jesus's efforts set the example for us to make the necessary changes today if we're going to save lives. So, it's on us, who claim to love our young men, to find different ways to bring folks a better understanding of who they are and who they can become.

Our young men desperately need to understand the transformation which happens when a person comes to accept the Lord. Through learning about their faith, young men will realize a belief in God can become their strength in a difficult situation. Everyone has power because everyone has gifts, and we cannot tell children this and then not know how to show them how to access these gifts. Parents say my child has gifts or my child is gifted. You need to teach them how to use those gifts because every child has something they are active at, something they are gifted in doing. God gave only to them and maybe a few others. You must go in there and find it. You must ask for his help, but you must know he taught us to turn to

Him. Many of us are not trained to worship, to praise; they are something different. Praise is celebrating God; worship is committing to Him. In church, most of us were shown how to glorify God, but we weren't instructed on how to worship within the faith. We weren't given actual plans; we weren't taught this is what the day looks like, what the fight will look like up close. For many of our young me, this is going to change when they become teenagers. They need to know this is what praise and worship are going to look like and how it will feel. But the increase of distractions is drawn them further away from the faith. It is in the young adult years we lose most our sons and daughters to all forms of religion. They will have to face another change when they move into adult life.

We cannot blame the children when they are born blank slates; it is what we allow them to become. That is our fault. If you let your child watch, God knows, how much television, you cannot now blame them because they don't speak properly and act the fool. You allowed that. If your child watches T.V. for hours, shows like *Love and Hip Hop* instead of reading is your fault for any deficiencies they develop. If you cannot understand, it is your fault. I do not blame children, but I do try to fix them before society punishes them for what they do not have, which is what typically happens. It is not about believing in God. If you do not believe in God, it is fine, but my question to you is how you have been able to do just doing for you? I can tell you when I lived for myself, things did not go the way I thought they should, but when I started a Godly focus, I started to understand life was about serving and helping others, great things began to happen. I have had some adverse situations, but my thought process, my focus, bad beliefs had changed.

I got tired of being selfish, misogynistic, hating myself and the way I treated others for being bored and lonely on the inside. I had everything around me. I got tired of feeling empty.

OUR BOND IS OUR GIFT

I filled an emptiness with the love of my girlfriend (now my wife), God, and my children, not in that order. It was admitting to God I was wrong, going home, and coming clean. It was admitting I had been cheating, and then wanting to repair things with everyone, and letting go of the darkness which made me who I was up to that point. Just because it is what you were born into it does not mean it's where you should remain; it just means you have a harder starting point than most people. We all have obstacles placed in our path. We all must force our way past these challenges, some of which are set in front of us by others. In the end, you control your actions. You may realize you should remove yourself from the vicinity of family and many others to fix yourself first then go back and save them.

Joseph needed to be in Egypt to find out who God wanted him to be before he could take care of his family, and it was his family which did him dirty, so he had all the reason in the world to be angry. But instead, he needed to be turned into a slave, put in jail, treated as if he raped someone only for him to eventually become almost as important as the king. Do you think Joseph knew at the time sitting in jail, for a crime he did not commit, he would later become second to the King of Egypt, which happen to be the largest nation in the world at the time? That is how God thinks. If we focus only on how we feel, we will never get to where God wants us to be. We should say, "God, I know you see all this, so I am just going to keep pushing forward because I know you have something better for me somewhere, maybe not here."

I am going to be very honest with you; some may not gain in this lifetime. It may be when you get to the other side (heaven), and God says to you let me show you what I have for you. We should believe there is more out there for us. Some people say this belief is foolishness because you are giving up your life now. I, however, would instead hold tight to my faith then be wayward and out of control down here only to find out I was wrong. Only to learn there is indeed an a price to be paid for personal wrongdoings. You can choose whatever you want. I'm not trying to influence anyone; I have a hard enough time trying to do the things I need to do.

Our job is to lay the road and get out the way while allowing someone else to use it. It may seem like we don't get credit for what we do, but we do because we know we did it and did it well. We can take pride in knowing this if we are going to change the lives of young men. With the resources available within churches if done correctly we can alter the destructive path many of our young men are on.

The Schools

What are our young men learning, who is doing the teaching, and do those in control have these young men's best interests at heart?

In my last school of almost one-thousand students, I was the sole male teacher of color. Total, there were only two male teachers. Where is the modeling supposed to come from for these young men and women, so they can see how a good, reliable male is supposed to carry themselves? I presented a puzzle analogy earlier, and I must repeat it here. In life, our young men do not have a puzzle box complete with the image of a robust black male role model. Without that picture and without the people around them teaching them how they should act, react, and treat others, our young men will give up trying to put the puzzle together because it is too complicated. Many of us keep looking at them, frustrated, asking, "How come you cannot figure this out?" And in anger, our young men respond, "Because you are not showing me *how* to figure it out."

OUR BOND IS OUR GIFT

I have a lot of students who came into my classroom, and they were fearful because they felt they didn't know where their strength laid, what their talents were. My job was to make them feel comfortable and to help them understand the blessings they possess with all the skills necessary to be able to do well in this class and the world. However, for that to happen, they had to be willing to meet me halfway, they had to trust me as the professional who cared about their growth, and in return, I was going to believe them to be the high-level students I was sure they could become.

When you have built trust with your students, you cannot betray their faith in any way. You must remember always to do what you said you're going do and mean every word. An educator should give the students ways to use strategies, gifts, and talents they possess. Gaining their trust and being able to offer them lifelong knowledge is where you earn your money as a teacher, not just for standing in the classroom.

When I walk into a classroom, I do not know exactly where my children are going to end up. I placed the bar high for them. I see them in the place there are in now, and I work hard to equip them with the tools they will need to succeed—currently and in the future. Although I don't try to predict where my students will end up; the beauty of being in teaching for over twenty years is I get to see kids I had when they were thirteen or fourteen years old who are grown, men and women. They now have children, and say to me, "Mr. B, I loved your classes." I have them on Facebook, and I get to see how their futures play out. One of my students is in a video where he learns he got a full ride to NYU. Let me tell you how God works. One of my former students from the last school I worked in for the New York Department of Education is now in college. She cannot stop telling people I am her former teacher. It makes me feel old. Another of my former students was the mother of a young man I was currently teaching. It was a pleasant reminder of the blessings granted to me over the years of teaching.

I taught Health Education and Physical Education, and I filled in as an English and math teacher, and I was the dean of students, so when you act out, they brought you to me. I am not a drill sergeant, but I am not someone you want to play with because I do not deal with games, and head games do not work with me. I see the world as it can be, but I never stop looking at it as it is. That double vision allows me to be who God created me to be. If you do not believe in God, you believe in the talents you have, whether you think God gave them to you or not. I believe our abilities are God-given. It is still the innate talents you have which can lead you away from adverse situations you come across. Many of our youth do not believe they have these natural abilities because their parents did not teach them or help them explore these skills.

And neither did anyone in the schools.

So, at the beginning of this section, I asked, *what are our young men learning, who is doing the teaching, and do those in control have these young men's best interests at heart?*

Having people from the schools on the team enables us to get answers to these questions and to understand where we must further develop the schools' action plan to help uplift our young men.

The Law and the Politicians

I cannot conclude this chapter without talking about *the law* and *politicians*. You will notice from the previous sections—the family, the church, and the schools—were extensive, and there is a reason for that. The people within these groups help to create the nucleus, the essence of our young men. They help to form the foundation for every young man. Those within the law and political realm affect this foundation, in significant ways. They shape and direct the societal issues our young men find themselves in. For law enforcement to understand our young men's lives, it is vital for them to open the doors to have conversations which share personal experiences an understanding from both sides. The police officers, detectives, sergeants, sheriffs should be a part of the team to help alleviate the fear young men have of them. This fear fuels their anger from what they see happening in the neighborhoods. Law enforcement must help change this for the greater good while building stronger ties between them and the communities to which these young men reside. If those of us who are part of young man's foundation building slip up on our job, our young men can find themselves in the grips of a law system which is not set up for their success. And this is also why it's important to have those within the political arena on the team: the mayors, governors, senators, representatives, city council members should support political ideas which include young men of color instead of allowing them to reach prison faster than college. Sadly, the world expects little of our young men of color. When those low expectations trickle down from those who govern society and those who control law and order within society, the need to protect and care and instruct our young men should become much more necessary.

Our Communities and Final Thought

It is a natural response to be angry when you feel underrepresented or silenced. One thing I have always worked hard to do is to listen to children. No matter what I was doing at work, if a child spoke, I stopped everything and listened to what they had to say. Even if the child is all over the place with their thoughts, I looked to help them to get to the heart of their problem, especially our young men.

Many of them have a hard time articulating how they feel because they are angry. These young men are mad because there is no representation of themselves in their daily lives. They're exposed to everyday situations, often, with no fathers in place at homes. We know to repair this problem resources must be secured. Again, this comes from no representation, no modeling, nothing to show them what they should be. When they can't find themselves, outside forces—such as societal norms and entertainment—will try to tell our young men who they are, what they are. We need to be able to examine those things which influence our children, find the triggers within that influence, pull those triggers out, and attach them to what we are trying to do. If our children give into the streets, intense music, and animalistic urges to feel good about themselves, we need to offer an alternative, a better option then. We cannot take away the things our children are serious about and not replace them with something as appealing as the original negative influences. We must keep in mind, trying to scare a child straight only works for so long, if at all. At a certain age, you cannot control a young adult with fear. These changes are part of the reason why law enforcement needs to be at the table to at least try to explain to our adolescent men problems need to be fixed now, so they are not behind bars later. A healthy fear of consequences early on is not a bad thing. Threatening is.

There needs to the be a discussion which covers every facet of a young black man's life. Each person who is affected by these young men needs to be at the table to discuss why our young men are angry.

It is not just fathers not being in the home.

OUR BOND IS OUR GIFT

It is not just single mothers having to raise young men alone.

It is not just schools not providing, teaching, or caring about the representation and well-being of young black men.

It is not just the churches who don't seem to care about the lives of our young men six days out of the week.

It is not just cops who seem to kill them at alarming rates.

We should take all those outlets and find the people connected to each who want to do well and then funnel our money into them. Before we can ask these children what they need to make their lives better, we need to make sure we have our resources in place and then place those resources into things that are eventually going to help change things for everyone. It means getting out your head and looking to assist others, which is very difficult. Loving wide open is a radical act. Do you know how brave you should be to open your heart and say I love you and mean it? On top of that, one must be comfortable with the fact there may be no return of the emotion shared. It is one of the most challenging things you will ever do. Therefore, so many of us are out here hurting one another—because the fear of being real and showing our hearts is too much to risk. However, we should risk making the connection and share love because it is the love which will bridge the chasms of age, gender, ethnicity, pain, and hurt to make things better for each child.

The world can be grimy, and it is our responsibility to erase the griminess—for ourselves and others.

When a brother walks up to you and says, "Yo, fam, look at that chick's behind," you must speak up and say, "Yo, she is someone's daughter, wife, and girlfriend. Don't talk to women like in that manner."

We must hold ourselves to a standard and hold others to the same high standard as well.

We all need accountability. When two people come together with the same agenda and work to make sure they keep up their words and actions to fulfill a plan, which is a blessing. We all get tired, we all grow fearful, we all have worry and doubt, and having an accountability partner who will be there to cheer you on, tell you the truth, and help you push on to the finish line is vital to your journey.

We all have pain, but we encourage each other by sharing our pain. Carry a bucket of water 20 feet, then back another 20 feet, your arms are going to hurt. But if someone comes over during the first 20 feet and takes the bucket from you and carries it half the distance for you so you can rest, you are going to be relaxed and less tired. You can do more because someone has helped lift your load. When we don't have someone in your life, you don't need to carry your burden alone. Carrying such negatives can cause pain to build within us, ultimately pushing out into anger and negative emotions and actions. We can see when someone or something is angry. Watch animals, your pets. Watch a baby when they are hungry or when they are sick. Pain manifests in our physical appearance, whether we try to hide it or not.

If we feel we don't have someone to go to, someone to help lift our load, there is still no reason to believe you must carry it alone because you always, *always* have God. We go to him and say, "Okay, God, I don't know what else to do," and immediately—if we are open to it—he gives us peace over our circumstances.

I reached this moment years ago in a hotel in Deep Water, New Jersey. I was down here in this hotel room waiting for a young lady to show up to share in my plan on infidelity. She was someone I should have never been back with due to the fact we've been caught before after an affair. When things did not work out the way I wanted that night, I became angry because I was not going to be able to have my way. I had driven all this way and set up this elaborate plan to cheat on my girlfriend, now wife, and it did not work the way I wanted. I realized I my anger grew because I had not dealt with my pain. I had a master's degree, the pretty girlfriend at home, and a nice truck. So why wasn't I happy? The answer was simple, I had not dealt with my internal pain. There was a brother, a fellow teacher I worked with, who always reminded me he was a Christian, and at one time, he used to be on drugs. My partner would often share with me how God saved him from the negatives which dominated his life. At the end of each school day, before we parted, he would say to me, if I turned my life to the Lord I would become an influential person for God. I would chuckle because it seemed so unlikely, but in that hotel room, feeling angry, and realizing my anger was connected to an unresolved pain I had yet to speak of in my life. I did the only thing which came to mind: fell to my knees, broken, and talked with God about this pain. I asked him what did he want from me? What did I need to do to fix this and remove this emptiness?

I received a response. Deep inside my body, who I believe to be God. It was a faint voice which appeared inside my being. The voice said "Get up. Go home and fix my home."

I called my grandmother, someone who was a praying woman and said, "I think I just heard the Lord's voice. What do I do?"

My grandmother said, "Do whatever he told you to do and leave me alone. Why are you calling me?"

Even in that hard love, she gave me; she was 100 percent right. She said if God told me to do something, then I already knew what to do. There shouldn't be a need to call her to ask. After talking to my grandmother, I called the brother who never stopped reminding me he was a Christian. He immediately told me to join him at Bible study because now I had heard the Lord, I needed to learn who God was so I could follow him.

I did that, and I have never looked back since.

Now as a man of God, I share my testimony everywhere in the hopes of inspiring others and letting them know you can go from the bottom to the top of your life. But it is about planning now, applying. It is one thing to come to God, it is now about learning how to live a daily soul, how do we make this work in our everyday planning, how do we make this work to fix others who are hurting? We must share what we know and have been through; we also must sit down and plan. This is when you hear people say faith without work is death. You can love God all you want, you can enjoy Jesus all you want, but if you do nothing, you are like an Elijah in a cave; you are just sitting in there fearful. The first thing God said to him was "Why are you in this cave?" We have young men are out here killing each other. Why? We need to deal with that. Why do they feel it is okay to take a life when just one life is so precious?

Our young men are angry because they are confused and scared. They see the situations going on around them and know they are powerless to do anything about it. So, what do most of them do? They give in to anger because that emotion has been proven to be financially and emotionally beneficial to them. Violence has been a way to keep them warm at night when dealing with the problems of their neighborhoods. Anger helps them protect their brothers, sisters, cousins, and the bum called dad or step in their eyes, who may or may not work. Aggression keeps them safe when traveling from their house to school because they may go through six or seven people who would love to hurt them just because their clothes are clean or newer than their own. They display a look of aggression so the person who might harm them goes, "Nah, they look like they might be hard to deal with." The young men then breathe a sigh of relief as they get to the school. Once these young men make it to school, they have to take another deep breath. Now they have to manage their anger in class because now they have to worry about being picked on or bullied for not having $200 sneakers or only having two uniforms they regularly wash to get through a school week.

So, what are we supposed to do? It is not just a singularity; it is a multi-tiered problem which can be fixed, but it won't get repaired by sitting and begging the Lord to change the circumstances for us. No, even God requires we get work done. We must get busy and hold ourselves and each other accountable for our actions. The truth is all of us in this environment are angry; it is not just the youth. This is the crazy part—we ask why young black men are mad, yet young single mothers are insane, as well. So are the fathers who are doing what they are supposed to be doing but who are mistreated because of the no good baby making fathers. Children who come from good homes and must protect themselves from children from adverse environments who do not know any better are angry. We're all angry when you consider the damage done and lives lost.

What counters the anger we're all feeling?

The answer is love, a sound plan, a soft word, and actions represent giving to others, not taking from them. Because anger is a reaction to something, we can fix the violence. And if we can see the rage, there is still an opportunity to mend and heal our young men.

Young men being angry are only a symptom. The whole point of all this is we should look at all the stimuli and look to fix it at one time. With repairing things at once, we can start to cut down on the variables which would create anger and problems. If we just focus on one aspect, young men being angry, is only focusing on the headache. We should focus on what is creating the problem, why whatever is creating the trouble is in place and what can we do to change, alleviate it or get rid of it. We should support each other by creating sound plans for and with each other and allow each other to at least see it is working. We should be open to saying this is what I believe; this is what I have done, this is what I am doing. But we should search out others.

Dr. Harper and I had a conversation two summers ago, and during that conversation, she told me about a project she wanted to write. I told her if God said she should write it, then she knew what she needed to do. She later wrote the book and returned to me, wanting my help with developing her book into a sturdy finished literary product. Previously, we had worked with a friend of hers, a graphic designer named Marissa (http://www.Facebook.com/BrittonDesignPalace). She completed a cover for a different author who contacted us. The beauty of it all is each person involved shared a connection to the Christian faith. The godly synergy here is pure; we all have similar values. I help Marissa in what she is doing as a designer; she takes the information I give her and brings it to others who are going to help build her business plateau. Because Marisa introduced me to Dr. Harper, she and I made a connection, and eventually, we published Dr. Harper's book *A Profit to Your Husband (*You can find at http://www.drmelindaharper.com) through our publishing house. We all are growing the Kingdom of the Lord. Here is the beauty of it all: Dr. Harper and Marisa were in Tennessee, and I was in New York. The internet allows us to remain connected to serve each other's needs. I haven't broken bread with Dr. Harper or Marisa, not yet, but we will. Using technology, we continued to build our godly connections with each other. Dr.

Harper has used her book to open doors for herself. She is using her book along with her business knowledge and expertise to help people in Tennessee and across the net. This way, people can learn from her book and work on their marriages and other aspects of their lives.

This is what we must do for each other to see growth in our communities. We must, whether face-to-face, virtually, or both, build relationships that create positive changes where we are.

If we get out and use the technology to speak to others about what our platforms are, if you do the things you are trying to do, be the change you want to see, then God will start to align the people up whom he needs you to build A a connect. And this is especially true for reaching out to our young men because these boys were born in the digital age; they are very well-versed in the tech lingo. To reach them, we need to stand in every space the kids are known to use to communicate with one another. When we take our stand—something we should do because Jesus said we should—we can use those spaces as a bridge to communication, and through this discussion, we can help our young men.

Who did you help today? This is a real and serious question. Do not go to bed without having helped at least one person, and if a person can be one of our young men, all the better.

At the start of this chapter, I stated six types of people we should bring to the table to start planning for the betterment of our young men. If we get at least three people from each category at our table to commit to connecting with each, it will allow 18 people to be positioned to make changes. I know it seems like pure math, but in many of these communities, you can't find anywhere near those numbers of people ready to help. My vision is simple; if those 18 people connect to 10 people each, will make 180 people. Now imagine, if those 180 people just reach two people each, and on and on. This outreach is how I would love to see people come together to change the urban landscape.

Two-hundred, three, four, or more soldiers is not an army; it might be considered a regiment, and I have seen the movie after movie show how one regiment shaped wars, how one regiment saved thousands of lives. With face-to-face and digital interactions, I know we can connect groups of Godly folks, mindset folks and do the things we need to do.

It is not as difficult as you think; it just means a commitment to change.

We must find those who are willing to commit to change and heal their home, then move outward to their street, then their community, their city, their state, etc.

We must find those who are willing to commit to not only supply their talents and knowledge, but also their money—as much as they can—to the cause of exacting positive change to all the spaces where our young men travel.

The following are self-reflection questions to journal your thoughts or to sit and think about the content in this chapter. Give yourself a quiet space to read, think, and write on these matters. And be honest with yourself. Honesty and transparency is the key to you getting to your best self.

Self-Reflection

Bonding with Our Young Men

"I believe children are our future. Teach them well and let them lead the way."

OUR BOND IS OUR GIFT

Writer Linda Creed knew the truth when she wrote these beginning lyrics to "The Greatest Love of All" in the 1970s.
Our children and their development are vital to the success of our future.
We acknowledged in the previous chapter our men need healing.
Unfortunately, there are many of our young men who need healing, too. And if they don't need the cure, then they need the understanding of what it means to be good men and live, work, and love productively and positively in society.
The most significant takeaway from this chapter is the need to bring people to the table can help in uplifting our young men. And this is something we ALL can do.
Take some time to think about the many spaces you travel through within your day. Think about the people you may know and the people your people may know.
Even if you start with only one person for each group, your small team can make a difference.

For your life-changing group, you will need:

•Someone from the family unit; Mothers, fathers, our young men, their siblings, grandmothers and fathers, aunts, uncles.
•Someone from the church; Clergy, Pastors, ministers.
•Someone from our educational systems; Teachers, administrators, principals.
•Someone from law enforcement; Police officers, detectives, sergeants, sheriffs.
•Someone from the political arena; Mayors, governors, senators, representatives, city council members.
•Someone from the community; Those leaders, such as doctors, nurses, social workers, lawyers, non-profit organizations,

or activist. Anyone who does essential work within the community.

Once you have your list of people, then you should work to spend time talking about the issues from each of these groups affect young men, and move into creating goals, writing plans, setting up mini-goals, and doing the work to help our young men.

OUR BOND IS OUR GIFT

They Are Still Out There

Part 1: The Good Man

Inspired by my friend author Phoenix Rayne (www.Facebook.com/PhoenixRayne)

There are some excellent men in the world.

It can be hard to believe when you're constantly bombarded with the wrong images of men, mainly via the internet.

In this digital age, we can find ourselves hooking up with people we talk to on websites, chat rooms, forums, and social media outlets. And we all know of the horror stories which come from meeting someone who seems too reasonable to be true only to realize the person wasn't really who they appeared to represent

The problem isn't there are no good men. The problem is discerning the bad from the good, which can be difficult. Developing this discernment can be difficult when you meet a man online. I know many of these online locations seem like fantastic spots to meet someone. But, I am going to tell you, as a former whore, these types of sites allowed me to manipulate situations and relationships so I could hide every flaw I had. The women were not sitting across from me to see my face as I lied, which worked to my advantage. I could become whatever they needed me to be because they would share enough with me in conversation I could cover up a lot of my evil intentions.

Let's say you meet a man online.

OUR BOND IS OUR GIFT

You see his picture and find yourself physically attracted to him. He sees your image, and the attraction is evident as well. Right at the start, the game is set into motion.

After perusing each other's profiles, you both learn you have many things in common, physical attraction, similar interests, and such.

The conversation would follow, and with the fast-paced growth of relationships online, the two of you would move into face-timing, live streaming, etc.

On your end, you think things are going well, and a real relationship might grow from these digital beginnings. A man, on the other hand, is a predator. He uses the internet to meet women like you—women open to love and relationships. His goal is to use technology to deepen his skills as a liar while creating multiple digital personas which would draw you in and keep you close.

Men like this are going to ask about your past relationships and hang-ups. They are going to listen intently and respond in a caring way. They'll learn and understand you do not trust easily and men have caused you to feel a little uneasy. Through these conversations, these types of men learn what will keep you close to them before they get physical with you. There might be a part of you which wonders about their intentions. You will think they're nothing more than smooth talkers. But there will be a more significant part of you admits this, having someone who listens is exactly what you've been waiting on, finally someone who gets you.

And yes, he does get you—because he *created* it to seem this way.

How do we get around all this? How do we get back to the realness of connecting with someone, sharing our needs, and exploring where we might go from here?

K.L. BELVIN

One thing we can do is realize past processes of creating relationships still work. We get so caught up in the quickness of our digital society we often forget the old practices can make for new and better connections. Think about how our grandparents met, dated, and got married. Consider how they built long-lasting lives together. Most of them courted each other by spending a lot of time getting to know one another. I would offer this, my sisters, please watch how a man treats his mother and sisters. This observation is old school yes, but still useful in uncovering a man's thoughts on women. Then examine how he acts in public. You should meet and look to have real conversations with men, considering who they are at the core. Listen to their platform to see if what they are saying is too rehearsed. Do not listen for the usual hiccups from friends of "oh does he have a ring on his finger"; he is going to know to remove it from the start. Start to look and see if what you are reading ads up to what you are listening to and with all of that, go on the next date.

As you are examining those past processes, make sure to include **spending the time** in the methods. Yes, we live in a "you can have it your way, right now" society, but taking time often reveals the marks of someone not right for you. It is the easiest way to weed out the pimps and the players. In finding your mate, saying you don't have time will not cut it. If having a healthy relationship is essential to you, then you will make the time to invest in the relationship.

When we move too fast, the crash can be disastrous.

If you take your time, you can go on several dates, have deep conversations, see a man in his environment, in action, and see if his words and actions match. Don't let the initial attraction, desire cloud the truth of who a man is.

If you meet a man and within a short span of time, he is sending you vulgar, sexual texts to test the waters, you should step back, examine the situation, and then flee the situation. Those messages are a sign he is not respecting you as a woman, and because you recognize yourself and know what you want, spotting men who try to strip you of respect should be more comfortable to do.

Now the real question is, do these types of men change? Yes, they do. I am an example of a whore getting his life together; it's something I wrote about in my book *From Gigolo to Jesus*.

I had the education, the beautiful woman at home, the jeep. I was thirty-six at the time. Once I realized I was screwed up, I had to learn to let the pain go. One pain I had to deal with was growing up without a father. Two years later, I reached out to my father and wrote him a simple letter; I told him I forgave him for everything he did, and I didn't hold any malice. I realized holding on to malice about him not being there was only keeping me from who I was becoming for the Lord. I sent him all of this in an email with some pictures of Tiff and my children to show him my growth as a man. You see, I was creating the difference I needed in my life.

My father said he read the email one hundred times because it touched him seeing the words and the pictures since we had never seen each other before that moment. He had thought my mother planted negative thoughts about him which had poisoned the water between us; she hadn't. A year after sending the email, I was sitting across from my father. You see male whores do change their lives, and you can find a good man if you make sure you're paying attention—and if you make sure, you and the man you are interested in being transparent with each other.

One of the things which captured my attention was a strong woman. I am talking about women who were comfortable with themselves to such a point they did not give into my foolishness. I enjoyed the type of women who did not allow me to control the situation because it was what I wanted. I found I enjoyed women who could control me because they did not allow me to control them. Every pimp, player, or panty hustler who is about his penis loves a woman who is in control of herself. It's a big turn-on. Many men quickly fall into trusting these types of a woman because her goal isn't to get sex or money. It's about whatever she wants, and she isn't scared to say what she wants in a man. My sisters, this is how you flush out the real man behind all the lies and virtual foolishness.

Once you have gained his trust, he will keep you close. And it will seem to him he has no choice but to follow you close because he wants to love you. When you have a man in this position, he will have to acknowledge what you want and what you need. He will look to take his place as the man who will lead you because his trust for you will be there. He also knows he won't be able to trick you into lowering your standards.

OUR BOND IS OUR GIFT

Part 2: The Good Woman

During the recording of the video this chapter came from, I was talking to my dear friend Phoenix Rayne, and during our conversation, she said she didn't trust people or men. I listened to what she said, and I felt compelled to share with her: Stop saying you do not trust people. Remember, words matter. If you continue to say you don't trust people, you will convince yourself this true, and in return, you will draw closer to you what your negative words attract: negative people. Instead of saying you don't trust men, say "I have met men who have given me a reason not to trust them, but that doesn't mean I distrust all men because there are men out there I know I can trust."

If you keep saying I do not trust, you will build a wall so high a real man will not want to come close because he is going to think to himself, is she or this relationship worth climbing this wall of doubt.

We must change what we say.

If you are Christian and pray to God and believe in him, then you know he is not going to send you the right man until you are the right woman. By taking a self-inventory, you can make time to work on you, to be in control of you. And when you do this, the right man will come, and he will sit across from you and know there is something different, unique about you—without you even speaking a word because your presence will exude your renewed self-worth.

A real man wants to hear your feelings about yourself because he knows this is what he is going to have to deal with if you guys date. A real man is going to sit across from you and

OUR BOND IS OUR GIFT

want to try to fix certain things which are wrong. He doesn't want to try to heal everything because he understands the energy it takes to do so. You are not his wife, he is not going to do that, but he will help you out with some things because a real man already knows the clowns are out here making it difficult for him. Therefore, he is going to come to the table open to some things; he is going to keep some things to himself because he should make sure you are the person for him. A real man is going to say, "I am not sure what I want regarding getting married right now." He will say, "I want a wife, but I am not ready to be married at the moment." When he says these things, what he is saying is "I want to see if you are the right person, so I am not going to take you down that road yet."

You must have real conversations; I call them business conversations. When you sit down and discuss your book with the editor, with the bookstore, you do not sit there and worry about what the weather is, how sales have been. You want to know what is going on with your book. You must take care of your personal the same way. You need to sit across from a man and say hello to set a stage which places both of you as equals. So, if you do come together, you will make a more significant pair than you would have ever been as individuals.

The union is what it's about, two people respecting each other, and respect coming from how you carry yourself.

And don't think you as a woman are the only one dealing with negative people. The good men you are looking for, live in the same world you do. Many of these men are dealing with the same foolishness you are dealing with because they are dealing with sisters who are uncomfortable with themselves, who have been hurt by stupid men and carry pain around with them.

From the center of my heart, I am sorry for every tear a good woman must cry because of bad relationships with an immature clown of a man. I want you to know the damages can stop and good times can arise in the future—if you value yourself and your time, set your standards, keep your head held high and walk in your truth.

Don't carry the pain of a bad relationship into the next one. Letting go is something we hear often but can't seem to release discomfort. The pain will do nothing but weigh you down and keep you from shining like the right woman you are and can be. You cannot heal if you are going to continue opening a wound as it starts to recover. No way possible. You cannot love God and love the pain because God is not pain. If we believe we are here for a purpose, then why would we hold on to baggage other people created or other things we allowed other people to do? Understand you cannot stop a man from lying, but you can control how it affects you, how much you will enable him to see you.

You don't want bad relationships to affect your trust or how you respond to new men. There are some women who, from being in a lousy relationship, carry knee-jerk reactions to everything new men do. Because the last man cheated on you, you are always waiting for the other shoe to drop in the new relationship, waiting for the cheating to start. As you become hyper-aware of all his actions, you can make yourself sensitive to everything he does. If he makes a mistake it wouldn't threaten a stable relationship, you might flip and break it off, thinking, "See, I knew he was going to do something." And for fear of feeling this small thing will turn into something significant and devastating, you flee the scene.

When you know your worth and only accept those in your life who not only value your worth but have their self-worth, then you are working from a place of right balance, sound foundation. There will be bumps in the road, of course,

OUR BOND IS OUR GIFT

because no one is perfect. Not you. Not the man who will be your happily ever after.

And it's so important to remember this. When you search for perfection, you are searching for emptiness because we all know perfection does not exist. We say it to each other on a regular basis. So, if you see yourself doing this, you cannot try to hold men to this standard.

What you can do is hold men to the standards you hold yourself too. If you keep yourself to a high standard and make strong demands of self, then any man who approaches you, talks to you, deals with you, and wants to be with you will understand why the bar doesn't get lowered. If you're a women of standing will find there is no reason to raise the bar simply because a man approached you. You'll stand firm on where you want it to be. Where that is for you, you'll decide in how you choose to carry yourself. We are human; we're all going to make mistakes, poor choices. We've heard this numerous times, but it is are daily choices which dictate who we become.

I am now a great husband because of the woman I am married. In my former marriage, I wasn't right for my wife, and she wasn't right for me. In the type of union I had with my first wife the only possible outcome was failure. We didn't know how to please or build each other up.

Now, I have a good woman who works with me on being the best man I can be, so I work to remain that man. She has proven herself to be the woman I need. Because of whom she is and what she brings to the table I fight to continue to be the best man possible even on days I may not feel like it. This happens because she continues to keep the bar high and has kept a high expectation of me and her. In 1995 when we first me the bar was set just as high and she was secure in who she was then. Five years later, in 2000, when I ran into her again she was the same woman only more mature. Tiff's robust and unwavering persona was important in condition my thoughts about how to act around her. She required me to move the same as she wanted me to five years early. She was not about the foolishness then, and she was not about the stupidity the next time I met her. You should control you; it is indeed the only thing you, or any of us, can do. This focused will has a fantastic effect on how brothers act. Then when you deal with men, make sure they understand what and who they are dealing with. You are a child of God. There is no reason to hold on to any past pain from any situation, and anyone who tries to convience you do so is not a positive force in your life. They shoud be showing you love will heal all pain. Before you can share the love of two being together there needs to be the love of one: self-love. This type of love is the key to positive and healthy growth. Once you live with an understanding of looking to increase love for yourself, you will not accept anything less.

Most of us have read the story of Ruth, and we understand the work Ruth put in. But what people tend to forget about Ruth is she lost her husband, two brothers-in-law, and her father-in-law. But she stayed firm, took care of her mother-in-law, and put the work in, and it was through the work Boaz saw in Ruth and said, "yes that is the woman right here. She is out here doing the job when there are just men out here". Then he put the word to the men around him, do not touch her leave her alone. Even when you are not paying attention, a good man is, a good man sees what a good woman is doing and wants to protect her. A moral man knows when a moral woman is putting in work, he understands. A man on this level knows how hard the grind is, so when he sees you grinding, he respects it because he knows what to he expects from himself when he gets up early in the morning to put in work.

OUR BOND IS OUR GIFT

In Ruth's story, another man had a shot at her, but he said he wanted nothing to do with her. Boaz was quick to react. He wanted Ruth because he knew what type of woman she was. The other man only knew about her history. He knew women from Moab were loose and nasty women. All he knew is what was shared about Ruth, but he never actually learned who she was or seen her in the fields at night.

Ruth did what she needed to do to keep her mother-in-law and herself alive, and she did it without complaint or reward. But she was rewarded when Boaz claimed her for his wife. Her tragedies had been restored many times over.

When you do the same, you will receive the same. When you work from a position of love, diligently putting forth the effort, you will attract people who are doing the same things you are. This positioning will cause what you are looking for to gravitate toward you. Your spirit will release radiant energy, and the spirit in someone else will say "I see a woman who's making things happen, I need to get to know her.

One exercise I want each of you to do is look in a mirror and do not leave your reflection until you see the beautiful woman you are. Yes, you are going to have to do like my girl, Viola Davis, from the T.V. series, *How to Get Away with Murder*, did when she took the wig and makeup off. You have to do the same when you are in your house. Remember no one will see so feel free to take the time to truly get into the natural you. Take off all your accessories off, as well, and see the beauty in being a woman. The accessories enhance the beauty that is already there. But if you need the accessories to feel beautiful, then something is missing in that mirror. Take off everything. You must learn to love every inch of who you are. You want him to enjoy every inch. If you are uncomfortable, he is going to be nervous and stumble around, trying to figure out how to make you comfortable or look to take advantage of your short comings. He is going to say to you there is nothing wrong with you being naked, I like seeing you that way. He is going to tell you there is nothing wrong with how you look; you do not need the wig. But if you're tied to the accessories, you are going to feel you are not yourself without them and miss the chance to create a lasting union.

Look in the mirror and find the beauty God gave you. It's there.

Find your beauty before the wrong man steps to you and tries to define who you are—and you begin to believe him.

When a man says he loves how you look, you should be thinking, I do, too.

When a man says he loves your nose, you should be thinking; I think that way about myself all the time.

When a man says you have a great smile, you should be thinking, that is one of the things I do while I am in the mirror all the time; I cheese all the time.

If you cannot see your beauty, he can tell you anything. If you do not believe you're beautiful, he will imprint any feelings he wants you to feel. This is his way of attempting to turn you into a puppet while he remains the puppet master.

Cut the strings and take control of yourself. Stand in front of the mirror in your raw nakedness, flaws and all, and find the beauty. Know there is a beauty. If you cannot see it the first time, tell the mirror you will be back tomorrow. Before you put on your accessories, stand in front of the mirror again and go, "My cheeks are not too bad," is a start, or "I have cute ears." Do it until you can say, "I am beautiful. I am sexy. Every inch of me is beautifully made."

When you get there, you become radiant, and the radiance is what men attract them.

Do not give up on believing good men exist. And do not give up on thinking you are a good woman, a beautiful woman

OUR BOND IS OUR GIFT

who is worth the best. It is the latter belief that will attract a real man to you.

Below are self-reflection questions to journal your thoughts or to sit and think about the content in this chapter. Give yourself a quiet space to read, think, and write on these matters. And be honest with yourself. Honesty and transparency is the key to you getting to your best self.

<u>Self-Reflection</u>

Bonding with Good Men and Women

It might be hard for some women to believe how they perceive themselves and their past relationships and the words they've consumed from others can negatively affect their ability to find and keep a good man. The same can be said for men looking for good women.

The four reflections below move you from thinking about yourself as an individual to thinking about yourself as a mate and how communication can affect that connection.

To bond with the right man or woman within you.
1. Understand who and what you are as a man/woman.
    a. determine if that understanding is good or bad
    b. find ways to eliminate the bad aspects and replace them with good ones
2. Decide on your worth and what you bring to the table of a stable relationship.
3. Examine what you need from a mate to create and sustain a stable relationship.

4. Understand how your communication (to self and others) can positively (or negatively) attract good men/women to you.

OUR BOND IS OUR GIFT

Folks Better Work It Out!

Here's a question to think about: if you want a relationship, are you going after it?

To obtain anything, we should start with two steps:
1. Understanding what we **want**.
2. Developing a set of actionable objectives/goals to get **want**.

Many of us know what we want—deep down. And some of us even know how to go about acquiring what we desire. What often trips us up, however, is the fear of sitting across from the person we genuinely wish and expressing to them precisely what we want. We might fear the rejection. We might worry about having to explain what we can offer to a great relationship.

We let previous relationships and bad situations keep us from pursuing our heart's desire.

We often talk about what we want, but we don't take the time to ask ourselves, "What am I bringing to the relationship table?"

Both parties in a relationship need to be active participants. They also should be mutual visionaries. They should be able to look at the future and see how they can tackle it together. They should understand what is out there for them, and then they must come up with a backup plan is going to protect and honor each other while still allowing each other to go after what it is they want. There is no room for hurting or disrespecting each other.

OUR BOND IS OUR GIFT

In addition to being active participants, both parties need to work on building a spiritual foundation for their relationship because there will be tests: tests by your family, your friends, your work, your children, etc. However, you will be able to withstand those tests if you and your mate have a healthy relationship with God.

Now, if you know these two things – being active and having a healthy spiritual foundation – are essential components to a healthy relationship, you should take a close self-inventory and ask yourself what you might be missing. People like to say their mates complete them, but the truth is you need to be complete within yourself to be whole within an association. If you are not honest about your deficiencies and how you might correct them, you will set yourself up for a bad relationship.

When thinking about good relationships, marriages, I tend to think about one of the unique days for a couple: the wedding. I think about this because I wonder how so many people forget this important part of the marital vows: "Let no man put asunder what God has put in place." God has placed you together, so no man can mess this up. Why do you lose the meaning to these words?

One thing I've noticed is when two people know who they are and what they want, and they form a beautiful union to conquer the world together, people are drawn to them. There's no more powerful force than a happily married couple. Therefore, so many people love former President Obama and the first lady. This is why so many people love Will and Jada. They love seeing them together because people like to look at other people in love.

When people see my wife and me giggling and playing, they come over and ask how long you've been married. We both work hard to be more than just words; we want to be *active*. I want people to see my wife on a pedestal because I put her there. I want folks to see my wife on high because I protect her while she's there. I make sure other men understand so if they even think about talking to her when I'm not around, they would to climb that pedestal first, and when others see her, they'll say to their significant other, "That's how you're supposed to treat me." One of the final reasons I place my wife on a pedestal: is so, I am reminded to live by example and encourage others to treat their mates with the same devotion.

I mentioned deficiencies earlier. When we don't come to a relationship altogether, when we enter the relationship full of shortcomings, adverse situations can arise, such as cheating.

When something is missing – something spiritually, physically, financially, and or sexually – people start looking in other places for fulfillment instead of going to their mate and being transparent with their feelings.

As we know by now, transparency is vital to a relationship. When you have a significant other, and the two of you are locked in together, and your focus is transparent and tight, there isn't a stronger force on this planet.

But first, you must overcome yourself and your weaknesses. You should be stronger than the fight-or-flight response we typically pursue. Many of us don't like confrontation. We don't want to hurt others or be hurt, so we flee dangerous situations in search of better.

But the better could be at the end of fighting through a situation. It's easy to leave, and it can be devastatingly hard to stay. It's hard to stay with someone who cheated on you. It's hard to be with someone who hurt you. It's hard to stay with someone who's as broke as you are. It's hard to go through the negativity when you're looking across the street at the next

OUR BOND IS OUR GIFT

person and thinking, "Their body is so much better than my significant other."

You should do the work. You must talk about the things which are lacking, the things you want. When you start working on mutual visions, as you begin to climb the ladder, the loving gets better. When the two of you are working on something, and you can see it all coming into play, there is no greater force on the planet than the union between happy wife and husband. You can't wait to get home to celebrate what you two have been together. It's those moments which ground you in such a way that when the negativity comes, you'll fight that much harder not to lose the good you have.

When you have a union of this magnitude to don't want taken from you or given away. Something inside you knows you can't live without them. So, cheating is not an option. Your thoughts are not to be on giving up real love up for just sex, for a new relationship which you don't know the outcome, is not likely.

In this excellent relationship, you are trying to build; you also need to understand each other's value. One thing couples tend to misunderstand is who should take the lead in a relationship. In may, cultures men are taught the man should be the leader. Yes, a man should protect his woman and provide for her, but he doesn't have to be the one to take the lead. Is it okay if the man offers comfort and protection, and his wife makes more money than him? Yes. Because in a relationship, it's not about *him* and *her*; it's about *them*, as a unit.

It hurts me when I hear couples arguing over things like sex, money, children, timing, quality time, romance, chores, and pet peeves. These types of arguments tie back to the need of a strong spiritual foundation. Having foundation keeps these issues from tearing a union apart. Imagine having the opportunity to do something incredible, and doubt settles in because you lack a solid grounding in a relationship. You begin to worry if you can accomplish the task of fixing these issues. We all know uncertainty and worry have a power to them which often defeats us. When you have a strong spiritual foundation, the anxiety from various problems can be doused with a few kind words from your mate or internally from your spirit.

When you secure your spiritual positioning, your level of concern for each other will flow back and forth between you. When issues arise, you can go to your mate when you have a problem and ask, "Baby, how am I going to handle this problem?" When in a great spiritual and emotional place, your mate will respond, "The way you do everything else, baby. You'll find a way to get it done. I am here if you need my help. We got this." That one response, those words of encouragement and belief in your abilities will make your heart pump faster and cause ideas to overpopulate your brain. Your eyes will widen as your back straightens. "You know what?" you'll say. "You're right." And you'll know your mate is right because if you have them in your corner, all will be well. This is what a spiritual covering looks like when your foundation is firm in your relationship, and vice versa.

I will tell anyone I am blessed to have my wife in my life because I know she will never lead me astray. She always has my best interest in her heart, and she's not afraid to tell me what she needs and wants from me.

And this goes all the way back to the first time we met. Her transparency, her strength showed me who she was, and I had to either come correct or not come at all.

While attending the college, I was married to my first wife, unfortunately, I was still doing every bad thing you could think of, including cheating. During this time, I met my current wife. She was 19, and I was 28. I asked her to go out with me to the movies, and she said yes. Everything had been going well between us until she asked, "Are you married?"

"Yeah," I replied, and she barely let the period end my response before she let me know she wanted nothing to do with me.

Five years later, my marriage was over, destroyed. I remember I was on track and saying, "Lord, just send me someone who understands me." I did not even ask for love, just understanding because I knew how difficult it was to deal with how nasty I was. What I did not know was that same night Tiff had prayed to God and said, "Send me someone who loves me" because she was tired of dudes who seemed to lack that ability.

It was then we reconnected. I attempted to talk to Tiff, but the first thing she said was, "Are you still married?"

She was a woman who stood her ground. A woman who knew her worth and knew what God made her be. Not some "other woman." Not someone willing to do whatever to satisfy a desire, to include bedding another woman's husband.

By her knowing her worth, all foolishness and pretenses disappeared.

I didn't try to lie or be sly with her. "Yes, I am," I replied, "but I'm separated, pending divorce. It's over, I'm back home with my mother and grandmother, and I'm trying to start my life all over again."

I was honest, and she walked into that honesty, but she was in no way naïve. She held her standards high, and as a result, I had to raise my game. We began talking again, and after she saw that my actions mirrored my words, we could have real conversations. We've been together ever since.

Was everything perfect hardly? I did not completely change my wicked ways at the start. What did make me align myself with Tiff was a choice she gave me: *you either should choose the hoes in the street or God and me*. I made my decision – to have her and God – because I knew her worth to my life.

Words gave us the ability to talk and share our thoughts, but it was the actions that showed her I could be what I said I wanted to be, what I said I wanted *us* to be.

You want to be a quality person in a stable relationship with a right person. You then need to say and act the same as the person you plan to connect with. By showing similar behavior, you attract the type of person who wants to be with you. You should live the life you say you want and then trust God will send that individual to you, and then the two of you should sit down and talk. Ask each other what you want. See if those wants to connect in a meaningful way. See if you both have a plan to make those wants reality.

Don't waste time playing in things that won't bring you your best life because time doesn't wait for any of us.

Below are self-reflection questions to journal your thoughts or to sit and think about the content in this chapter. Give yourself a quiet space to read, think, and write on these matters. And be honest with yourself. Honesty and transparency is the key to you getting to your best self.

Self-Reflection

Bonding while Working It Out

At the start of this chapter, you read the following question: if you want a relationship, are you going after it?
The chapter states:

OUR BOND IS OUR GIFT

To obtain anything, we must start with two steps:

1. Understanding what it is we **want**.
2. Developing a set of actionable objectives/goals to get to that **want**.

In your reflection of this chapter, the above steps are what you should start. What do you want, really want? What do you envision when you think of your pursuit of relationship happiness? This vision could also be on obtaining a career or personal goal.

What actionable objectives will you complete to obtain this want? If you are not doing these things, you will not accomplish the goal of happy content relationships.

Remember, place strong action behind your intentions, desires, and dreams.

About the Author

Keith "K. L." Belvin is an author, counselor, educator, mentor, and public speaker with over twenty years of educational experience with the New York City Department of Education. Keith is happily married to his lovely wife he's bonded with since 2000 and married in 2007. Keith and his beautiful wife currently live in Dover, DE, where they are raising their precious daughter Kayelle, named after her father. He's Big K. L., and she's little Kayelle.

His background includes an MA in Human Service Counseling/ Specializing in Christian Ministry from Liberty University, an MS in Education/Specializing in Curriculum Writing, Assessments, and Teaching from Walden University, and teaching credentials from the states of Delaware and New York. Keith has appeared in Ebony Magazine (February 2012) and Black Expression Book Club. He has been a guest on national radio shows such as Hot 97 FM NYC, Power 105 FM NYC, and on television shows such as The Rick Sanchez Show on CNN.

Through his private counseling practice, Keith has helped many singles and couples in developing actionable goals to becoming better individuals and mates.

He is also the founder and operator of Bravin Publishing LLC, a company who provides literary services to new and upcoming authors. Established in 2010, Bravin Publishing has released all of Keith's titles as well as 40+ other titles from other authors.

OUR BOND IS OUR GIFT

All of Keith K. L. Belvin's titles are available on his company's, Bravin Publishing LLC, website. www.BavinPublishing.com

- **Our Bond is Our Gift** (Personal Development)
- **Lukewarm Saint** (Inspirational Fiction)
- **From Gigolo to Jesus** (Autobiography)
- **A Man in Transition** (Poetic Anthology)

K. L.'s other titles are available on the Bravin Publishing website.

- **Wordplay 1: Words are our Canvas 2012** (Poetic Anthology)
- **The Soul of a Man Part 1** 2009 (Inspirational Anthology ft. African American Men)
- **The Soul of a Man Part 2** 2016 (Inspirational Anthology ft. African American Men)

***With The Soul of a Man, if not ordered from www.BravinPublishing.com you are not ordering from Keith "K. L." Belvin's company and he will not receive the royalties from the purchase. ***
For a 20% discount on your purchase from the Bravin Publishing website use discount code **KLBelvin**.

www.ingramcontent.com/pod-product-compliance
Lightning Source LLC
Chambersburg PA
CBHW070738020526
44118CB00035B/1476